# Ethics for Architects

# Ethics for Architects

## 50 Dilemmas of Professional Practice

# *Thomas Fisher*

**Princeton Architectural Press, New York**

The **Architecture Briefs** series takes on a variety of single topics of interest to architecture students and young professionals. Field-specific information and digital techniques are presented in a user-friendly manner along with basic principles of design and construction. The series familiarizes readers with the concepts and technical terms necessary to successfully translate ideas into built form.

Also available in this series:

**Architects Draw***:*
*Freehand Fundamentals*
Sue Ferguson Gussow
978-1-56898-740-8

**Digital Fabrications***:*
*Architectural and Material Techniques*
Lisa Iwamoto
978-1-56898-790-3

**Building Envelopes***:*
*An Integrated Approach*
Jenny Lovell
978-1-56898-818-4

**Architectural Photography the Digital Way**
Gerry Kopelow
978-1-56898-697-5

To my father, who first sparked my interest in ethics, and my mother, who showed me how to live a good life

Published by
Princeton Architectural Press
37 East Seventh Street
New York, New York 10003

For a free catalog of books, call 1.800.722.6657.
Visit our website at www.papress.com.

Editor: Dan Simon
Designer: Jan Haux

Special thanks to: Nettie Aljian, Bree Anne Apperley,
Sara Bader, Nicola Bednarek Brower, Janet Behning,
Becca Casbon, Carina Cha, Tom Cho, Penny (Yuen
Pik) Chu, Carolyn Deuschle, Russell Fernandez, Pete
Fitzpatrick, Linda Lee, Laurie Manfra, John Myers,
Katharine Myers, Steve Royal, Andrew Stepanian,
Jennifer Thompson, Paul Wagner, Joseph Weston,
and Deb Wood of Princeton Architectural Press
—Kevin C. Lippert, publisher

Library of Congress Cataloging-in-Publication Data
Fisher, Thomas, 1953–
Ethics for architects : 50 dilemmas of professional
practice / Thomas Fisher.
p.  cm. — (Architecture briefs series)
ISBN 978-1-56898-946-4 (alk. paper)
1. Architects—Professional ethics. 2. Architecture—
Moral and ethical aspects. I. Title.
NA1995.F57 2009
174'.972—dc22
                              2009036440

# Contents

**Introduction**
— 10 —

# 1
## *General Obligations*

**Conflicts of Interest**
— 17 —
**Uncompensated Work**
— 19 —
**Community Service**
— 21 —
**Pro Bono Work**
— 23 —
**Living Conditions**
— 25 —
**Working Conditions**
— 28 —
**Layoffs**
— 30 —
**Unequal Pay**
— 33 —

# 2
## *Obligations to the Public*

**Repressive Governments**
— 39 —
**Corrupt Politicians**
— 41 —
**Public Officials**
— 44 —
**Public Opinion**
— 46 —
**Public Bailouts**
— 49 —
**Public Reviews**
— 52 —
**Public Health**
— 54 —
**Cultural Differences**
— 57 —

# 3

# *Obligations to the Client*

**Self-Destructive Behavior**
— 63 —
**Distrustful Behavior**
— 65 —
**Dishonest Behavior**
— 68 —
**Deceptive Behavior**
— 69 —
**Spendthrift Behavior**
— 72 —
**Solicitous Behavior**
— 74 —
**Unrealistic Expectations**
— 76 —
**Manipulative Situations**
— 78 —
**Deceiving a Client**
— 81 —

# 4

# *Obligations to the Profession*

**Greed**
— 87 —
**Insensitivity**
— 89 —
**Jealousy**
— 91 —
**Betrayal**
— 93 —
**Treachery**
— 96 —
**Unfairness**
— 98 —
**Uncertainty**
— 100 —
**Cheating**
— 103 —

# 5

## *Obligations to Colleagues*

**Office Affairs**

— 109 —

**Working Hours**

— 111 —

**Labor Law Violations**

— 113 —

**Crediting Coworkers**

— 116 —

**Accommodating Disabilities**

— 118 —

**Firm Bankruptcy**

— 120 —

**Firm Loyalties**

— 123 —

**Untrustworthy Colleagues**

— 125 —

# 6

## *Obligations to the Environment*

**Environmental Hypocrisy**

— 131 —

**Environmental Conflicts**

— 133 —

**Contextual Conflicts**

— 136 —

**Social Justice**

— 138 —

**Future Generations**

— 140 —

**Other Species**

— 143 —

**Reducing Waste**

— 145 —

**Reducing Consumption**

— 147 —

**Rights of Nature**

— 150 —

**Postscript: Why Ethics Matters Now**

—152—

# Introduction

I began my architectural career with an ethical dilemma, when a firm agreed to let me work for them—for free. Still in school, I needed money, but I also needed the experience, and so I accepted their offer, aware of the unfairness of it, not only to me but also to others who could not agree to such terms because they depended on summer jobs to pay for their education. That experience introduced me to the way architectural offices worked, and it also initiated my interest in the ethics of professional practice, which led to this book.

Like most people, architects want to do the right thing. That is often easier said than done, however, as I show in the case studies that follow, which are based on situations that I have encountered directly or have heard of from colleagues. In each case I try to sort out the most appropriate response, drawing from the four major approaches to Western ethics: what it means to be a good person (virtue ethics) or to have a good society (contract ethics), and what is the right action in terms of the individual (duty ethics) or the group (utilitarian ethics). A tabulation of the four approaches might look like this:

|  | **Good Character** | **Right Action** |
| --- | --- | --- |
| **Individual** | Virtue ethics | Duty ethics |
| **Group** | Contract ethics | Utilitarian ethics |

These four approaches to ethics relate to four of the phases of architectural projects: pursuing and attaining the commission, assembling the team and signing the contract, developing the design and contract documents, and administering the construction and close-out of the project. Although all phases of an architectural project can raise a diversity of ethical dilemmas, each phase tends to draw more heavily on one approach to ethics more than others.

The gaining of a commission often depends as much on the character of the architect and the chemistry between the client and designer as on anything that the firm has already built. Here, virtue ethics, with its emphasis on character traits such as honesty, integrity, and fairness, can make the difference between an architect and client developing a good working relationship or not.

Upon receipt of a commission, though, the architect's command of contract ethics becomes more important. The negotiation of the rights and responsibilities of different parties, the heart of social contract theory, plays itself out in the agreements between architects and clients, as well as in those between architects and consultants. Doing this well, without antagonizing others or disadvantaging ourselves, makes all the difference between good and bad relations in a project.

The design and contract document phase demands yet another approach: duty ethics, with its focus on good intentions. Design, as we discovered in school, is almost entirely about intentions, about which Immanuel Kant urged us to ask: Have we treated others as ends in themselves or simply as a means to our ends? Likewise, during the detailing of projects, we should ask ourselves how reasonable and attainable a solution to a problem might be. Is it, as Kant would ask, universally valid or not?

Then, as the project progresses into construction, utilitarian ethics become increasingly relevant. As we administer that process and bring the project to a close, we need to ask questions about the consequences of what we have created. Has the project benefited the greatest number of people, and has it addressed their pragmatic needs?

If ethics has relevance to every part of an architectural project, so too does it relate to every part of the architectural curriculum, even though the discussion of ethics too often gets relegated to just the professional practice course. This undervaluing of ethics has skewed the way we view our responsibilities. Too many architects, for example, rarely return to their buildings to conduct post-occupancy evaluations to assess the long-term effects of design decisions, revealing a certain blindness in our profession to the utilitarian demand that we attend to the consequences of what we do. Likewise, too many of us excuse the egomania of our most honored colleagues, showing how little we seem to care about virtue in our profession, with its emphasis on good character as the basis for doing good work. Nor has our profession been particularly politically active, putting relatively little of our leverage behind changing the unfair economic structures and social contracts within which we operate and to which our buildings often provide support. At the same time, the scrutiny we place on the intentions of students in studio and architects in practice indicates how much duty ethics has pervaded our discipline.

Over the last century, we have created a lot of "architecture of good intentions," as Colin Rowe observed, while paying relatively little attention to the character of our colleagues, to the nature of our social contract, or to the consequences of what we have built. Extending our appreciation of ethics beyond good intentions to include other approaches—virtue, contract, and utilitarian ethics—remains one goal of this book. Extending the scope of our ethical obligations is another. Our responsibilities as architects need to go beyond our direct obligations to clients, communities, colleagues, and coworkers. The sustainability movement has revealed how much of what we do affects the public at large and those only indirectly affected by our decisions, as well as future generations and other species. That may sound so expansive as to make ethical decision-making seem almost impossible: How can we account for our effect on those whom we will never meet?

The answer to such a question demands a particularly important skill we learn in school: imagining what most people cannot yet envision. The empathic projection of how a decision will affect others over time remains one of the great values architects bring to problems, and applying that ability to ethical dilemmas offers a way to think about ethics across a wide range of social, spatial, and temporal scales.

Practical reasons exist for thinking about ethics this way. We can no longer afford to exclude other people, generations, or species from our ethical deliberations because, having done so in the past, we have begun to exhaust resources that we depend on, to extinguish species essential to our own health, and to exacerbate climate changes that threaten our very survival. We can no longer view the planet, and its many cultures, species, and generations, as externalities beyond inclusion in our moral calculations. Unless we start taking the good of all into account, we will have very little good left at all.

In that light, architectural education and practice would not only benefit from a greater understanding of ethics but also might benefit ethics itself. An architect's ability to think simultaneously at many different scales and to assess the value of alternatives that do not yet exist could broaden the scope of ethics, while also helping people find the most appropriate responses to the ethical dilemmas they encounter in life. Most unethical behavior stems from people seeing the world and their own interests too narrowly. Once they recognize how much each of us affect and are in turn affected by myriad others, it becomes clear that the most ethical path is also almost always the most practical, the most economical, and ultimately the most sustainable way forward.

This book has six chapters, following the six canons of the American Institute of Architects (AIA) Code of Ethics and Professional Conduct, published by the AIA General Council (Washington, D.C., 2008):

1. General Obligations
2. Obligations to the Public
3. Obligations to the Client
4. Obligations to the Profession
5. Obligations to Colleagues
6. Obligations to the Environment

The first five canons exist in order of scale, starting with the most general obligations and continuing to those that affect the greatest number of people, the public, to the fewest number, colleagues and coworkers. The sixth canon, a newcomer, addresses the environment, which covers the broadest scale of all, that of the entire planet. Since none of the other obligations makes a difference if we no longer have an environment that can support us, you could read this book from back to front, starting with the environmental cases at the end.

The AIA's code encompasses all four approaches to ethics. Its canons invoke virtue ethics to urge architects to "maintain and advance their knowledge...exercise unprejudiced and unbiased judgment...[and] respect the rights...of their colleagues." Contract ethics appears in such statements as "members should embrace the spirit and letter of the law...promote and serve the public interest...[and] serve their clients competently." Duty ethics emerges in lines like "[members should] exercise learned and uncompromised professional judgment...[and] uphold the integrity and dignity of the profession." Finally, we hear a utilitarian focus on consequences when we read that members should "thoughtfully consider the social and environmental impact of their professional activities."

An ethical code, however well framed or stated, matters only if those bound by it also enact it in their daily lives. No professional code of conduct can substitute for the determination of each of us to lead as ethically responsible a life as we can, seeing every dilemma we encounter as an opportunity to ask what constitutes the right thing to do, what will achieve the greatest good, and what virtues must come into play. Ethics, as Aristotle observed, must become a habit, so that we condition ourselves to the right kind of response to a situation, particularly when tempted by the often easier, unethical path. It may seem simpler to take a shortcut or take advantage of others, to act shortsightedly or selfishly toward others, or to ignore the rights of or our responsibilities to others. But such behavior always costs us dearly in the long run.

Unethical behavior is especially costly to professionals, whose real value and only true currency rests with our reputations and the respect and regard that others have for us. Every unethical act, every lapse in our character or betrayal of others' trust, constitutes a self-inflicted injury that can take much longer to repair than anything that we think we might have gained. As I hope you will see by reading this book, the ethics of architectural practice is really about whether we can sustain a practice at all. Good values, in other words, create the greatest value, and embodying that in everything we do needs to become such a habit that we no longer need to read books like this. Until then, I hope the examples that follow prove as helpful to you to read as they were for me to write.

# Chapter

# 1

# General Obligations

Members should maintain and advance their knowledge of the art and science of architecture, respect the body of architectural accomplishment, contribute to its growth, thoughtfully consider the social and environmental impact of their professional activities, and exercise learned and uncompromised professional judgment.

# Conflicts of Interest

**A nonprofit organization intent on adding to its facility had a wealthy patron on the building committee who had donated a lot of money to the project and who had a relative, an architect, competing for the job. Another architectural firm, asked to submit a proposal for the commission, had to decide if it was worth competing for the job, knowing about this apparent conflict of interest.**

Of all the possible ethical violations, conflicts of interest have become among the most obvious and most-often encountered in many organizations and professions. For-profit and nonprofit operations alike often require that employees regularly report any potential conflicts of interest in the execution of their duties. In this way, organizations hope to determine whether a particular conflict crosses the line, ethically, and whether employees should remove themselves from the situation or renounce the connection that could cause a problem. Professionals have to be especially wary of appearances of conflict of interest. The AIA's code of ethics addresses conflicts of interest in several places, not only in an architect's own practice but also in the actions of clients, manufacturers, contractors, and public officials. Professions, like corporations and governments, depend on trust to operate and have credibility, and few things undermine confidence faster than the appearance of a conflict of interest.

Nonprofit organizations have the added burden of dealing with this among donors. The bylaws of most boards address conflicts of interest, but rarely does that extend to those who have given an organization a great deal of money, often with an intended outcome in mind. In such situations, it may seem sensible to give the donor a voice in how that goal gets implemented, but that can cause conflicts in at least two directions. Philanthropy requires that the funds be given without too much direction from the donor, lest the donation violate the legal requirements of a tax-exempt gift. At the same time, charity demands that the donor not benefit personally, other than from the tax deduction that comes from making the donation.

The potential for both types of conflict exists in this case, in which a donor sits on a committee deciding on the architect who will use the donor's money to help build the building. Were the donor to influence the organization unduly in the choice of architect, a conflict of interest would arise not only in his role on the committee but also potentially in his role as a donor having made a tax-deductible gift. There are several options. He needs to report the conflict, in case some did not know of his connection to one of the competing firms, and he should remove himself from the interview of and deliberation over that firm. One of the first rules of ethics

entails honesty and openness when interacting with others. But recusing himself from key discussions of the committee also makes his participation on it pointless, and so the best course would be for those who assembled the committee to not place him on it to begin with or to remove him from it as soon as the conflict of interest becomes apparent, however awkward that might be.

What should the other firms competing for the commission do? They have no direct influence on the organization or its committee members, and lacking such leverage, they can simply take their chances competing in a process so fraught with potential conflict. But they have another kind of leverage, which goes to the heart of conflict of interest: telling the organization how the situation appears to others. Honesty remains the best policy in dealing with a potential conflict, not only internally but externally as well, and the competing firms have much to gain and little to lose in being as open as possible with the organization's leadership: if the donor is removed from the committee, they all have a more level playing field on which to compete, and if he is not, they would all be better off not competing against such odds.

Ethical dilemmas like this often revolve around the conflict, as Abraham Lincoln observed, between the love of property and the consciousness of right and wrong. Our course seems crooked and our conduct a riddle when the love of property gets the better of our reason. An acute sensitivity to appearances of conflict of interest is not just a nicety for the faint of heart; it is the best way to avoid being perceived as crooked.

# Uncompensated Work

**An architect had a developer friend who had commissioned her firm to design projects for him in the past, but who asked her to do some designs for him for free, unable to pay her because of the recession, but holding out the possibility of the work turning into a commission once things turned around. She found the project appealing and she had the time for it, but wondered what she might be getting into if she agreed.**

Because architecture, like all creative fields, has qualities of both a vocation and an avocation, as both a job and a calling, architects can find it tempting to design for free, often for the pleasure of doing so and in anticipation of a possible paying commission coming from it. The ethics of this depend on the degree of volition or free choice in doing such work. If done willingly, without feeling pressured, then uncompensated design raises no ethical issue; without freedom, as the philosopher Jacques Ellul has argued, there is no ethics. Ethics assumes we have a choice to act in one way or another, or else why bother to discuss it at all?

But rarely, if ever, do any of us have complete freedom. Freedom from all limits—negative freedom, as the historian Isaiah Berlin called it-remains something we might imagine, but almost never attain, since we all live within constraints of some sort. This makes determining the degree to which we have free will a more difficult task, one that demands weighing the intentions and consequences of what we "freely" do. In the case of an architect having to decide whether to provide some free design services to a friend and potential client, the issue involves not only the architect's willingness to do this work but also the implicit risk and responsibility she takes on in the process. Offering her advice on what her developer friend might do makes her a participant in and possible defendant of whatever moves forward, even if both parties cite a hold-harmless agreement. Professional licensure carries with it responsibilities that cannot be waived by any one individual, since it includes obligations to public health, safety, and welfare that extend beyond any agreement between two parties. The architect is never free of such duties, even when working without pay.

That shows how much a professional donates in providing free service. It becomes more than not charging for the time taken to produce the design; it also includes not accounting for the liability and the risk associated with the work, which can be extraordinary, depending on what the recipient of the services does with the results. The latter donation often remains invisible to people seeking professional advice and often results in architects, especially, being underpaid, even when compensated for their work. The legal responsibility that goes with creating something as costly and complex as a building extends far beyond what a typical fee covers, making liability insurance for architects fairly expensive.

For one friend to ask another to take on such risk without any reward, now or in the future, hardly seems like friendship. Likewise, the freedom to expose oneself to so much liability without any equity stake in the results hardly seems like freedom. If freedom, as Friedrich Nietzsche observed, involves being responsible to ourselves, then the real freedom of the architect here, asked to provide free design services to a friend, involves saying no. To do otherwise is to be irresponsible to ourselves and entails the loss of freedom as a result, as would happen should the freely given design fail in some fundamental way outside the architect's control and expose her to liability and litigation.

That other architects will provide uncompensated design services in hopes of winning a commission does not make it right or wise to do so. People relinquish their freedom out of ignorance all the time, as we see all too often in the political realm, but few will do so knowingly. Some might argue that we should be free to give up our freedom if we so choose, but that "positive freedom," as Berlin called it, has always been the means for a few to oppress the many. The test of real freedom and real friendship comes with turning the tables and asking for compensation in a form commensurate with the actual value of what has been asked for by those who request free service. In this example, the architect might ask of her developer friend an equal stake in the development, with enough control of the design to ensure its appropriate implementation. Anything less than that, and she should use her free will to turn down this opportunity. That's what friends are for.

# Community Service

**A**n architectural office relied on one employee to lead much of its work in the community. The firm touted his work in its marketing materials and told him how important he was for attracting more business from nonprofits and the public sector. When the next economic downturn came, however, the firm laid him off first, telling him that he did not bring in enough fee-paying work and that it could no longer afford him.

What is the price of community work, and when does it become too costly? The answer depends on what we mean by price and how we measure value. In our current economy, prices often exclude externalities, things of value that we cannot easily quantify and so do not get included in calculating costs and benefits. As a result, economic value does not always capture what we value as a community, society, or culture.

That, in turn, often places businesses in the paradoxical situation of reaping great profit from what we know to be the worst for us, whether it be gas-guzzling cars or nutritionally empty junk food or the addictive consumption of alcohol or cigarettes. At the same time, activities of real value—like mentoring youth or raising children or tending gardens—lie outside our economic system and so reap no financial profit, however humanly or environmentally profitable they may be.

Still, we admire those who give back to the communities from which we all benefit, especially in economic downturns, when the needs increase at the very moment that profits are down. As the psychologist Charles Garfield noted, what we really value becomes most clearly perceived not just in the best of times but also—and maybe even more so—in the worst. What we claim to value gets tested in downturns, when we have to set priorities and make decisions about what we can and cannot afford.

Community service usually loses out, since it brings in little—if any—money. As with this firm, the person most involved in such work was the first to be let go. But values provide perspective, as Garfield says, and so they help us step back and see our situations from a larger context and longer time frame. When we do that, we often discover that making decisions based primarily on reducing short-term costs almost always proves more costly in the long run.

It may seem less costly to tolerate people living on the streets than to build supportive housing for them, but it is not true. When we add up the expense of emergency room visits, the price of police calls, and the impact of criminal activity, it ultimately costs much more to have homeless people on the streets than to create shelter for them. The same can be said for other social ills we think we cannot afford to cure. Forcing the uninsured to use emergency rooms raises health costs for everyone else, and tolerating the high numbers of high-school dropouts eventually raises our costs through higher crime rates and more prisons.

Architects have a lot to offer in such situations, by revealing the real cost of doing what may seem most economically beneficial in the short term. We do this all the time with buildings, showing through life-cycle costing how a more expensive, higher quality product or material will save much more in the long run. But we—and almost everyone else—miss chances of doing this at a community or system-wide scale, especially during economic downturns. Recessions provide us with creative opportunities to see value often overlooked during a boom.

In the case of this firm, rather than see the person doing a lot of community work as the most expendable staff member, the firm should view him as offering some of the greatest potential for creating new business by showing communities how they can reduce costs or increase value in all that the economy has externalized. Tapping the often-unaccounted-for assets of a community—its people—in meeting needs or resolving problems remains one of the great areas of unrealized growth.

The same is true of firms. Employees remain a firm's greatest asset, and shedding people is almost always more costly in the long run. Better to devise alternatives—incentives or profit-sharing ideas for generating new work, paying benefits while putting people on retainer—than to get rid of professional staff altogether. Through such actions, we can show others how to create value that people often overlook while building, in the worst of times, on what we value most.

## Pro Bono Work

> Philanthropy is almost the only virtue that is sufficiently appreciated by mankind. Nay, it is greatly overrated, and it is our selfishness that overrates it. —Henry David Thoreau

**During a severe economic downturn, students could not find summer jobs, as firms furloughed or laid off a sizable number of employees. In one community, the unemployed students and practitioners decided to join forces to work, pro bono, on community projects, but several professionals raised questions about the ethics of students working on projects without pay and of the student-practitioner teams providing free service in competition with firms seeking paid commissions.**

Depending on the motives and circumstances, giving can be one of the best or worst things we can do. Thoreau captured that paradox in *Walden* when he wrote, "If I knew for a certainty that a man was coming to my house with the conscious design of doing me good, I should run for my life…for fear that I should get some of his good done to me." Everyone likes to receive a gift or an offer of help, but if given because givers want to curry our favor or assuage their guilty conscience, to put us down or signify their superiority, then we should, indeed, run for our lives. Giving done for the wrong reasons, to enhance the giver's power or ego, remains worse than not giving at all.

Immanuel Kant's ethical idea of treating others as an end in themselves rather than as a means to our ends serves as a guide here. Giving should benefit the receiver, not the giver. While giving offers a donor a personal sense of satisfaction, the act of giving has to arise out of what the recipient really needs or wants, and it cannot imply any quid pro quo—any expectation of a gift or even an expression of gratitude in return. The truest gift comes anonymously.

Likewise, the gift of our effort or example represents a benefit often far more valuable than what money can buy. As Thoreau rightly observes, "Some show their kindness to the poor by employing them in their kitchens. Would they not be kinder if they employed themselves there?" This giving of one's self has a particular relevance to professions like architecture. The doing of pro bono work for those in need, who lack the ability to pay an architect's fee, has become a growing part of the profession, with many firms now devoting one percent of their time to unpaid design services. Tax benefits do accrue with such work, so it does come with a benefit to the providers of these free services, but it typically involves giving their time to listen to the needs of others and to offer solutions to meet those needs.

Those who do pro bono work face two challenges. For architects worried that it will take away potentially fee-paying work, as in the example here, the donation of services can seem like a betrayal, an undercutting of one's professional peers especially if, during a recession, there is not enough work to go around. And, for the recipients, it can seem disempowering by reinforcing the position of professionals over those who have lost the ability to construct their own shelter or create their own place in which to live or work. Such resistance from both directions can make pro bono work seem not worth the effort, a damned-if-you-do, damned-if-you-don't proposition. But Thoreau's caution against the conscious design of doing good suggests another way to give that does not enhance the giver at the expense of the receiver.

Instead of widening the split between professional knowledge and the public's dependence on it, pro bono work should seek to heal that divide by teaching people to do for themselves what professionals have been empowered by the licensure to provide. That obviously does not work for a large, complicated project, the understanding of which demands years of training to handle its complexities. Most of what the poor need, however, is much simpler—shelter, storage, sanitation, security—and much more easily obtained with professional guidance. Helping people learn how to help themselves remains the greatest gift of all, for it frees them of needing any further gifts and enables them to give to others in turn.

Although this might appear to threaten the very idea of professional knowledge, we have plenty of restrictions in our regulations to prevent untrained people from doing things that might harm the health, safety, and welfare of themselves or others. What it does threaten, and deservedly so, is the false philanthropy that Thoreau speaks of. Rather than do good *to* others, we need to do good *with* them, helping others to no longer need our help. Thoreau did that in *Walden,* where he described how he built his own house so that readers could build theirs, and those among us who follow his model will never lack for meaningful, important work.

## Living Conditions

**Simulation, evocation, contextualism: call it what you will, but this thing that we designers are so good at seems to serve a basic human need.** —Michael Bierut

An architect led a study abroad trip with a group of students to Africa, where they intended to design and help build housing for a village. When they got there, though, they heard tales of the fishermen in the village drowning for lack of life jackets and children falling

# to their deaths in the well for lack of a lift mechanism. Although the architect and students did not intend to design life jackets or a lift mechanism, they did, since these were what the people needed.

An issue that has preoccupied ethicists over the last century involves the "fact-value distinction," most famously raised by the eighteenth-century philosopher David Hume, who argued that we cannot draw conclusions about what we ought to do in a situation from the facts about it. This presents, according to Hume, a problem for ethics, if evaluating what we ought to do has no rational basis. It also presents a problem for design, since designers constantly make decisions about what ought to be done in a situation based on the facts encountered therein. A particular group of people has certain needs, a site has certain dimensions, ordinances require certain things—and out of that welter of facts comes a design that addresses these demands while creating something of value.

Designers make this connection between facts and values through a number of non-logical means: simulation, evocation, and contextualism, as the designer Michael Bierut puts it. We model alternatives, suggest possibilities, and provide frameworks to help people begin to envision what they might have and really need. Those models and frameworks are, of course, facts themselves, even though they do not describe the world as it is, but instead as it might be and as the designer thinks it ought to be.

It may be that in science, charged with understanding the world as it exists, the fact-value distinction provides an important check on making sure an investigator sticks to the facts and does not let assumptions about what ought to be cloud the analysis about what is. But in design, which works almost entirely in the world as it could be, the fact-value distinction serves a different purpose, reminding us to make sure that what we value does not wander too far from the facts of a case or too far from the values of those we serve. Our ethical responsibility as architects involves making a fact-value connection.

That becomes particularly important when serving people of another culture or with very few resources, as is the case here. The architect and his students may have thought that they would go to that African village to design and build housing, but the facts—and the villagers' own priorities—said otherwise. Losing husbands to drowning or children to the bottom of a well trumps a better roof over one's head, and in such situations it becomes incumbent on designers to respond to what they see and hear and to switch gears accordingly.

Situations like this highlight a weakness in design education, which typically tracks students according to the end product they learn to produce. Architecture students learn to design buildings; industrial designers, products; apparel designers, clothing; and so on. While each design area does have its own history and skill set, all designers share a common discipline, a common way to perceive, analyze, and solve problems. We ought to be flexible enough to recognize the limits of our knowledge, generous enough to bring in other disciplines when needed, and open enough to apply what we know to problems outside our comfort zone.

At the same time, conditions such as those encountered in that village highlight a weakness in design practice, in which most professionals focus nearly all of their attention and talent on the relatively rich while almost completely ignoring the needs of the vastly greater number of the world's poor. It is as if we have allowed Hume's fact-value distinction to cloud our judgment. What we have come to value as designers—the custom designs we create for a fee for a relative few around the globe—no longer aligns with the facts of where the greatest demand for design creativity exists, among the billions of people who lack the most basic necessities.

When we finally figure out how to reconnect these facts with what we value, we may also discover one other aspect of Hume's distinction. Most of what we value in the affluent West and think indispensable to living does not jibe with the facts that we see in so much of the rest of the world, which shows how relatively little, in the end, any of us really need to lead a comfortable life.

## Working Conditions

An interior designer, refurbishing a number of hotels, found a supplier of handwoven rugs made in an impoverished country that cost much less than rugs made in more developed nations. Though the designer thought that her purchase of the rugs would provide needed income for the people who made them, she knew of the terrible working conditions of the rugs' weavers. She wondered if she should use her leverage as a buyer of a large number of rugs to improve the situation or not purchase the rugs so as not to enrich the supplier who allows such conditions to occur.

The design community has an enormous impact on the planet, not only in what we build but also in what we specify—the products and services we select as we put a structure and interior together. We generally focus on the end result of that process, on what a product looks like or how it performs, but the effect of our decisions goes far beyond the space of a building's walls or a site's boundaries. It also extends to the people who make the materials we use, whose lives we can improve according to what we do or do not select. Our purchasing power gives us leverage, if and when we decide to use it.

The ethical dilemma this creates for designers revolves around the question of whether to help change the working conditions of those affected by our decisions or to protest those conditions by not selecting the products of their work. Stoicism offers some guidance here. The ancient Greek Stoics urged us to not concern ourselves with things in the external world over which we have no control, with the goal of helping us reach a state of tranquility. The interior designer in this case might make a Stoic argument and rightly say that she has little or no control over the material conditions of the rugmakers and that she should not concern herself with their plight when making her decision about what product to specify.

Contrary to what Stoic ethics seems to suggest, though, we can never be entirely detached from the consequences of our actions. To select something involves taking a stand and, at least indirectly, supporting the conditions of those who made it, and it means nothing if we achieve inner calm at the expense of the agony of others. The

Stoic philosopher Epictetus distinguished between disruptive passions that cause us to lose control of ourselves, and the rational emotions, such as affection and sympathy for others, over which we retain control. This echoes Lincoln's observation that "the strongest bond of human sympathy outside the family relation should be one uniting working people of all nations and tongues." Reason tells us that we can improve the working conditions of people around the globe, as we have done in this country. Calmly going about making that happen remains well within our ethical responsibility as professionals and as human beings.

But would this interior designer do more by buying the rugs or refusing to buy them? Refusal may prove more satisfying emotionally, but by removing herself from engagement with those who have created the conditions she opposes, she also eliminates her opportunity to effect change, as well as possibly making the workers' situation worse by lessening the demand for their handiwork. At the same time, buying the rugs without comment does seem to condone what she otherwise condemns. Stoic ethics urged each of us to accept, calmly, the conditions of our lives, but it did not counsel us to tolerate the injustices of others.

Instead, the Stoics would advise her to do as much as is in her power to do. She could, for example, ask the supplier about the working conditions of his employees as part of her making a decision about the rugs, sending a message that it matters to her and to other customers. She might also suggest that she would be willing to pay more for the rugs if the company could show evidence of improvement to their worker's conditions or if it was willing to bring those conditions in line with the workplace standards in more developed countries. And, with the dispassionate calmness that the Stoics so valued, she could also let the supplier know that she will do everything in her power to encourage others to follow her in this until the company changes its labor practices. We should be emotionally imperturbable in the face of injustice, but never morally indifferent to it.

## Layoffs

In a country well governed, poverty is something to be ashamed of. In a country badly governed, wealth is something to be ashamed of. —Confucius

# The owner of a small firm needed to lay off one of two employees. One was a young, energetic recent graduate who had no dependents and a terrific work ethic. The other was a longtime employee with a lot of experience and higher salary, but who worked more slowly and with less energy

# because of medical issues that made him dependent on his employer-supplied health plan.

The most difficult ethical dilemmas often arise when our actions have life-or-death implications. The law deals with the most harmful situations, but it does not extend to perfectly legal actions, like a layoff, that can have the same effect of endangering a person's health through the loss of benefits. Lacking such coverage, of course, does not mean a person cannot get medical attention, evident in the large number of people who use emergency rooms as their primary clinic. And, if we pay enough, we can get all the coverage we need, although most people only face that situation after they have lost a job and have less money for more expensive insurance.

Such flawed public policies create ethical dilemmas for the owners and managers of organizations, as in the case here. The law may allow us to do things that we may feel violate the moral law, and so we have to work through that conflict both as individuals and as communities in the best way we can. In this situation, some may see little conflict at all. The firm's principal needs to look after the health and well-being of the business first, and if an individual suffers as a result of a layoff, so be it. In most cases, that would mean keeping the young, productive employee and laying off the less productive, more expensive one. But even the most rational and responsible business person remains a human

being as well, and the linkage of health-care coverage to employment makes every layoff decision much more difficult. It threatens a person not only with the loss of a salary but also potential bankruptcy and financial ruin should a serious accident or illness occur while he or she is unemployed.

Confucian ethics offers some perspective on this. Were our country well governed, we would all be ashamed by the impoverishment of people who have lost a job and become ill through no fault of their own. Good government would not allow something like this, affecting potentially everyone in the country. The bad government that has enabled this to happen is also a democratically elected one. We should never have allowed our elected officials to be swayed by those who benefit from our dysfunctional health-care system, maintaining something so hazardous to almost every citizen's own physical and financial health. Very well-to-do individuals—some of whom hold higher office and have become beholden to the health-care industry as it stands—may not have to worry about losing a job or paying for medical attention. But, given our government, the wealthy should be ashamed.

Whatever the politics of the situation, it does not ease the ethics of it. Confucius made a connection between good government and the good person, believing that the best leader ruled by moral example rather than through self-interest, and that the superior person behaved according to moral principle, in contrast to the inferior person's focus on profit. Such ethics, of course, runs counter to our profit-oriented economic system that assumes that everyone bases decisions on self-interest. It does show, however, another way to think about ethical dilemmas such as the one described here.

The Confucian ethical ideal involved the balancing of mutual obligations, and in that light, the head of this firm might explore a third way with his two employees. After explaining the firm's financial situation, he could ask the two employees to split one position, while offering to continue the health-care benefits of both. Since neither of his two staff members would know who would be laid off, both might accept half a job, with benefits, over no job or benefits at all. And if one did not and found another job, both would still have their health benefits provided. He might also provide an incentive for both employees to seek new business, offering to return each to full-time employment if they bring work into the office. Poverty is nothing to be ashamed of if it comes with the means to transcend it.

That cooperative approach contradicts the tendency of businesses to lay off staff in a downturn. Keeping as many people employed as possible, even if part time, not only encourages more of the familial and social harmony that Confucian ethics so valued but also bolsters staff loyalty and the incentive for people to work harder for the organization. Retaining some level of employment among as many people as possible also buffers an economic decline and hastens a recovery, resolving the cause of the problem in the first place. In the end, the best economy—and the best government—arises not just from self-interested competition but also from what Confucius called *ren*: compassion for others, which we hope that others will also have for us.

# Unequal Pay

An architect, well regarded in a firm, discovered that she was making less than some of her male counterparts who had less responsibility and less longevity in the office. Angered by the inequality, she went to talk to the partners, demanding that she receive more pay than her subordinates or she would quit. The partners said that they could not increase her compensation because of the recession, so she walked out, remaining unemployed for a long time and eventually taking another job with considerably lower pay and much less responsibility than what she had before.

What people get paid remains one of the most sensitive of issues, even though in developed countries and among most professions the pay we receive puts us all among the best-paid people on the planet. Compensation, in that sense, is relative to the context in which it occurs. While we might occupy the top tier of what people make in a world in which two billion people live on less than two dollars a day, we may feel impoverished in comparison with those who commission us or even with those who sit at the desk next to our's. Add to that the culture of overconsumption that bombards us daily with images of what it means to be wealthy, and we all can easily begin to feel poor, however well off we might be.

Differences in pay become even more difficult to accept when seemingly discriminatory in origin, when people of apparently equal ability receive more or less depending on their gender or ethnic background. Our legal system, of course, offers some protection from explicit discrimination along these lines, but there remain gaps in pay, with the 2003 U.S. census showing that for every dollar men earn, women earn 75 cents. Whether the result of marketplace forces or male oppression, the disparity shows that our economic system, for all its touted opportunities, lacks fairness at a fundamental level.

In ethics, fairness has been among the most valued of the virtues. The reciprocity inherent in ethical behavior, of treating others as we would want them to treat us, would suggest that men and women of roughly the same educational and skill level would receive roughly the same pay.

Architects enact such equality in what we design all the time. We typically create work or living environments based on people's needs and interactions, without ever making distinctions in the nature or quality of space—except in restrooms and other similar gender-specific spaces—between men and women engaged in equivalent activities. This occurs partly for practical reasons, since we rarely know who will occupy spaces over time. But it also arises out of an ethical obligation to be as fair as possible in our accommodation of others.

Fairness, of course, does not always mean absolute equality, since people are not absolutely the same, and this is where prudence, another virtue, comes into play. Fairness in accommodating differences can lead to varied conditions in some cases, uniform conditions in others. Building codes, for instance, have finally recognized the need for a larger number of restroom stalls for women, especially in entertainment venues when intermissions lead to an influx of people needing such facilities. At the same time, universal design demands that we adjust dimensions to accommodate the needs of people with a wide range of physical ability, with many elements of buildings lower or wider than what has existed in the past. Examples like this suggest that fairness without prudence can lead, paradoxically, to unfair conditions, and that true fairness comes only from imagining ourselves in the place of those often treated unfairly and responding to their needs accordingly.

That can occur in practice as well as in design. The architect in this case had every right—and a good deal of courage—to speak to her employers about the unequal pay she received for equivalent work, and about the inequality of her receiving less than those who had less longevity in the office than she did. The missing virtue here, though, was not just fairness but also prudence on both her part and on the part of her bosses. As Montaigne observed, "We undo ourselves by impatience," and her imprudence in leaving the firm in the midst of a recession as well as the partners' imprudent refusal to consider a salary increase for her, even if it needed to be delayed until the economy improved, reveals a degree of impatience that can end up reinforcing the very inequality that initiated the confrontation. The architect, in taking a lower-paying job, has fallen farther behind her male colleagues in her previous firm, and the partners, in letting her leave, have higher-paid employees with less experience than her.

Some might argue that she had a duty to leave, just as we can rightly say that the firm had a duty to adjust her pay, when it could afford to do so, in recognition of her ability and longevity. But prudence remains as much an ethical duty as the courage to speak out for equality, and sometimes the most effective way to change a situation lies in speaking up for what is right and then working from within a culture to change it over time. Misfortunes have their life and their limits, said Montaigne, and so, eventually, do inequality and unfairness. Through patient and persistent resistance to the latter, we can eventually achieve the equality and fairness that can otherwise seem so elusive.

# Chapter

# 2

# *Obligations to the Public*

Members should embrace the spirit and letter of the law governing their professional affairs and should promote and serve the public interest in their personal and professional activities.

# Repressive Governments

An internationally known architect received a commission to design a major public building for a government renowned for its repressiveness toward its own people and its aggressiveness toward neighboring countries. It would be an important project for the architect, although his peers criticized him for accepting the commission. The client has treated him well and has given him a great deal of latitude in the design of the project, and he has argued that doing a good building is his only ethical responsibility, regardless of what others think about the government's politics.

In a global economy, architecture has become one of the most visible ways in which clients, including national governments, can garner the attention of and generate a positive image within the international community. Buildings in such situations become symbols of a country's sophistication and savvy, and totems of a nation's aspirations and ambitions. Although it has generated a lot of work for architects, globalization has brought with it ethical dilemmas, as in the case described here. The ethical responsibility of an architect involves doing the best building possible, meeting the client's needs within the budget and schedule, while also attending to the health, safety, and welfare of those who will use or inhabit the structure. Yet it seems disingenuous not to acknowledge the larger social and political context within which we build, especially when it is clear that a client has commissioned a project as much for its symbolic importance as for its serviceable accommodations.

In some ways, architects have always faced this dilemma. Architecture remains one of the most expensive of the arts, and as such, its realization has often required the support of the wealthy and powerful, some of whom may have less-than-sterling records when it comes to how they acquired their wealth or kept their power. There is, in almost every society, even in those that democratically elect their leaders, a degree of oppression, as Karl Marx caustically observes. But architecture can play a somewhat subversive role in such situations. While the rich and powerful—whether individuals, corporations, institutions, or governments—most often commission architects, the ethics of the profession demands that we look out for the public interest, which may or may not align with the client's interests. In an inverse of the oppression Marx saw all around him, architects can help channel the wealth of a few to benefit the needs of many.

In the case of the architect commissioned by that repressive government, he could walk away from the commission and protect his reputation among those who find it offensive to do anything for that regime. In a world in which hundreds of millions of people lack even the most minimally acceptable shelter, there are certainly many other opportunities for architects to meet the expectations of licensure and attend to people's health, safety, and welfare. But it remains a viable—and ethical—option to keep such a commission and use it to create a nonoppressive environment for as many people as possible. Virtue ethics does not mean that we need to avoid nonvirtuous people at all times. Rather, it asks that we behave virtuously and that we refuse to let others force us to do otherwise. We cannot help it that other people—or politicians—lack virtue; we can only act in as virtuous a way as we can and hope that others recognize that, in the end, it remains the only path to meaningful success.

From that perspective, the architect here would be better off not declining the commission up-front but, instead, pushing the project as far as humanly possible to benefit the public and all of the people who use it through a design that embodies such virtues as justice and courage, honesty and respect, generosity and acceptance of differences. If the client prevents him from achieving such qualities, the very components of what makes a building "good," the architect should walk away from the project and let the oppressors oppress someone else.

## Corrupt Politicians

**Among a people generally corrupt, liberty cannot long exist.** —Edmund Burke

A public official lets it be known that payments to his reelection campaign will expedite the approval of construction projects in his state. He has structured this so that there is no obvious connection between the two, enabling him to deny any charges of corruption, but everyone in the industry knows that this is the only way to get approvals in a timely manner. An out-of-state architect hears about the expected bribe, and she

# must decide whether to look the other way or say something about it to her peers or the press.

Corrupt politicians and public officials have a long history of looking to the construction industry for payment or other perks to expedite projects. The pressures to complete buildings on time and within budget help fuel the bribery that has plagued the industry in the past. And the temptation of some to use their public office to seek advantage for themselves provides the oxygen that can ignite corruption, destroying any semblance of ethical behavior.

While bribery may seem like an easy way for a modestly paid public servant to make some extra money, it never works out in the end. Look at Spiro T. Agnew, the former governor of Maryland and Richard Nixon's vice president, who had to resign his national office when residents of his state sued him to repay money he had taken in bribes from the construction industry during his governorship. Agnew never again held a political position and, even after his death, remains a symbol of the corrosive and ultimately catastrophic effect of corruption not just in politics but also in construction.

What should this architect do when she hears about the need to contribute to a politician's campaign fund to help hasten approvals? The AIA code of ethics has a clear answer: "Members shall neither offer nor make any payment or gift to a public official with the intent of influencing the official's judgment in connection with an existing or prospective project in which the Members are interested." But does the same ethical obligation hold if this architect hears of bribes occurring in other projects or by others on her project not under her supervision?

Here, the law is clear. Architects, or any citizen, for that matter cannot remain silent if there is evidence of others breaking the law. Failure to blow the whistle makes a person an accomplice in the illegal activity, even if not directly involved. That may not seem fair, but as Edmund Burke observes, corruption ultimately affects us all by making liberty impossible. Our responsibility to the good of a community comes before our maintaining a working relationship with those who are not so good.

More than just political liberty is at stake here. Personal liberty—the ability to act freely and live by the consequences of our own actions—also disappears in the shadow of corruption. The effect that even the appearance of complying with corruption could have on this architect's reputation should alone be enough of a threat to prompt her immediate refusal to engage in bribery. Better to blow the whistle and lose a commission than go to court and lose her career.

A tradition of bribery in some places makes it harder to blow the whistle. What if the people this architect turns to have themselves been corrupted? Burke might have responded that unethical traditions do not deserve anyone's allegiance. While he valued tradition, he saw in the slow evolution of a community's values the filtering out of vice and the fostering of virtues that provide a check against corruption. Prudence and temperance show how stupid and self-defeating bribery can be, while courage and justice remind us of how important it is to call out corruption and to prevent it from poisoning our liberty. Once we accept public officials taking bribes, it becomes only a matter of time before we accept other abuses. A bribe may directly affect only a few, but it harms everyone in general.

The reasons to protest corruption go beyond the personal and the political. The very nature of professional activity rests on the conviction that we must speak the truth as we see it, however inconvenient or unpleasant it may be to some. Absent that, professions simply become a type of business, which in turn undermines the trust that society places in us through our education and licensure to look after the public good. Professionals rarely encounter situations like this architect, in which her speaking out is as necessary as it is difficult to do. But such occasions reinforce the reason why professions exist and why we enter them, upholding their ethics, in the first place. As Burke also said, "Nobody made a greater mistake than he who did nothing because he could only do a little." To do a little thing like blowing the whistle is to do a lot.

There are two things that one must get used to or one will find life unendurable: the damages of time and injustices of men. —Nicolas Chamfort

A state department of transportation hired an engineering firm many years ago to design a bridge as efficiently and economically as possible. That same department, over the next several decades, proceeded to add traffic lanes, raise vehicular load limits, cut back on bridge maintenance, and use the bridge to store heavy equipment and materials during repaving. Eventually, the bridge collapsed, killing many people, although in a subsequent report, the state blamed the failure on a design flaw by the original engineers.

Those in power often find it easier to blame others than to take responsibility for their own actions. As the eighteenth-century playwright Nicolas Chamfort observed, the "damages of time" and the "injustices of men" represent two of the inescapable aspects of life. We tend to think of injustice, though, as something immediate, but Chamfort's comment begs the question of how the damages of time and the injustices of men go together. Does time make it easier for us to be unjust to others?

The ethics of Epicurus offers some insight here. Popularly known for their exquisite taste, especially with regard to food, the ancient Epicureans urged us to focus on the present moment's limited pleasures, knowing how limitless desires can lead us astray. Constantly having more and doing more of what we want results not in more pleasure, said Epicurus, but only pain and sorrow.

The bridge in this case reveals the relevance of that wisdom. The structure's *fracture-critical* design arose from the desire to have as much bridge for as little money and material as possible. The engineers designed a highly efficient span, but one that lacked redundancy and so remained vulnerable to collapse if any part of it failed. Such fracture-critical design reflects the hubris or arrogance that characterized post–World War II America, where, having become the world's leading economic and military power, Americans too often acted as if we could do no wrong. As a result, we continually cut costs and pushed limits, out of an overwhelming desire for more.

That hubris became so endemic that it affected far more than bridge design. We have put in place a fracture-critical global financial system, in which the failure of a couple of investment banks set off a chain-reaction collapse of the credit and stock markets around the world; a fracture-critical transportation system, in which the dependence on fossil fuels compromises both our energy and our national security; and even fracture-critical suburban developments, in which the foreclosure and bank-sale of a few houses have led to the collapse in prices of all the other identical houses in a neighborhood.

The ethics here has to do not only with the pain and suffering such collapses bring in their wake but also in the shifting of one generation's debts and delayed investments onto the next, showing how injustice does damage over time. We have to take care not to do what the bureaucrats did in the case of this bridge, sloughing off their negligence by blaming the original designers who, after all, did what the state asked them to do. Whining about what our predecessors did not do for us becomes another form of injustice. But we should learn the lessons of Epicurus and not leave our descendants with the burden that comes from letting quantity trump quality, efficiency trump resiliency, and short-term gains trump long-term value.

Such behavior, as the Stoics would say, goes against nature. Fracture-critical design not only runs counter to the redundancy and resiliency we find in nature's healthiest ecosystems but also contradicts the natural tendency of most of us to want to leave a better world behind for our children. If it is unfair to blame our predecessors for structures we have not maintained, so too has there been a lack of prudence on the part of our predecessors for not anticipating changes that can compromise a design. To expect everything to work precisely as planned and remain in a perfect state of preservation flies in the face of all that we know about nature, human and nonhuman alike.

The prudent path lies in expecting the worst to happen and planning for it. In that sense, ethics and design require the same of us: to imagine the least desirable action or most disastrous outcome and to work through possible responses or alternative scenarios. Anything less leaves us open to blame by those who suffer the consequences of our hubris and who have to clean up what we leave in our wake. "Justice," as Epicurus said, "is a kind of compact not to harm or be harmed."

# Public Opinion

**Public opinion, though often formed upon a wrong basis, generally has a strong underlying sense of justice.**
—Abraham Lincoln

A bank wanted to build a new building for itself in a neighborhood's commercial center. The bank's owner liked the historic and architecturally significant public library on the next block and asked the architects to echo the library in the

**new bank building. The community, however, wanted a more modest building. The owner insisted that, as the client, he get his way, although the architects advised him to listen to what the neighbors wanted.**

The architect in this case faced a common dilemma, in which the desires of a client clash with those of a community. The resolution of such conflicts constitutes one of the real values designers bring to projects, since devising ways to resolve aesthetic disagreements can take as much skill as that needed to solve functional problems or to deliver a project on time and in budget. Design thinking involves the finding of win-win solutions to seemingly unsolvable problems, and architects, in situations like this, serve their clients best by listening to the conflicting opinions expressed about the initial design and using that information to refine the design. In this case, a number of ways existed to respect the neighboring library without mimicking it, seeking a balance between modernism and tradition, the iconic and the contextual.

But the conflicting opinion of people about architecture often has an ethical aspect to it as well as an aesthetic one. As Lincoln observed, public opinion may often be based on partial information, but a certain underlying justice remains in it. And as the writer James Surowiecki argues in his book *The Wisdom of Crowds*, numerous examples exist in which the aggregated insights of large groups of people can often lead to better decisions than those made by any one individual. Taken together, those two observations—that the opinion of large groups often embodies both justice and wisdom—lead us to an ethical virtue that is as controversial as it is essential to professional practice in any form of participatory governance: the virtue of tolerance.

The debate over whether tolerance constitutes a virtue revolves around the question of its limits. Is it a virtue to tolerate anything and everything, including intolerance? Aristotle's ethics of the median, embraced by modern philosophers such as Jacques Maritain, can help answer that question. It is possible to have a tolerance so complete that, as Maritain observed, it would lead us to deny even the possibility of agreement about the truth of a situation. Yet we can also encounter intolerance so absolute that it refuses to accept the position or even the very existence of those whom we disagree with or dislike. Between the two extremes lies genuine tolerance, says Maritain: an openness to the position of others whom we may disagree with and a patience with their position even if they have yet to discover what we believe to be the truth of a situation. True tolerance involves careful, attentive listening and the respect due to the opinions of others, however uninformed or misguided they may be in the end.

Surowiecki's wisdom of crowds reflects that idea. People must be willing to give each other the time for their opinion to be heard, knowing that, with enough input from as many sources as possible, the wisest decisions will emerge. Tolerance involves a respectful process, not an indifferent or incoherent result. And therein lies the value of tolerance for the designer. The architect and client in this case still had the right to design the bank, but they also had the responsibility to listen in an open-minded way to the community and to draw the best ideas from that input. Participatory processes like this may not produce brilliant design, if we measure that in terms of how much it reflects one person's vision, but they almost always result in the best design, one that addresses the valid arguments of others to create something better than what most people can imagine. In the case of this bank, whose depositors include many people in the neighborhood, accommodating the community's perspective in the design not only made architectural sense but economic and ethical sense as well. Every building offers a chance to construct what the philosopher Andrew Fiala calls the "tolerant community…in which participants recognize the limits of knowledge and share a commitment to engage together in the process of questioning, while allowing one another to disagree."

## Public Bailouts

Some people regard private enterprise as a predatory tiger to be shot.
Others look on it as a cow they can
milk. Not enough people see it as
a healthy horse, pulling a sturdy
wagon. —Winston Churchill

An architectural firm received a sizable commission by a major investment bank to renovate its headquarters. Shortly afterward, the bank began to have financial difficulties, ultimately receiving a substantial government bailout. The firm wondered if the project would proceed, but the bank told it to continue the work as planned. With a severe recession under way, the firm needed the work but wondered if the project could appear insensitive to possible public perceptions of extravagance and inappropriateness, given the bank's bailout by taxpayers.

In her book *The Shock Doctrine: The Rise of Disaster Capitalism*, Naomi Klein argues that the neoconservative effort to privatize the public sector led to the perverse situation in which the U.S. government created disasters to provide business opportunities for companies. She traces the rise of this "shock doctrine" to the University of Chicago economist Milton Friedman, who argued that "only a crisis—actual or perceived—produces real change." For Friedman and his followers, that change involved a radical diminishing of the public sector through "a rapid-fire transformation of the economy—tax cuts, free trade, privatized services, cuts to social spending and deregulation" in times of stress.

Klein's argument may seem far removed from the concerns of architects. We may find it distressing, as citizens and human beings, to think of our government manufacturing disasters as a form of economic development while largely ignoring the pain, suffering, and even death that accompanies human-created catastrophes. As professionals, our work toward designing a better physical environment appears almost the opposite of Klein's argument. Architects sometimes shock by creating important or impressive buildings, not destroying them.

Architects, however, have long benefited from human-made disasters. Look at the aftermath of Chicago's 1871 fire, San Francisco's 1906 earthquake, or New Orleans's 2005 flood. Although natural disasters in some sense, these three events show the extent of damage and destruction that followed from combustible building construction or crumbling concrete levees that arose from lax regulation or inadequate maintenance. Architects may

not intend to participate in disaster capitalism but participate we do, nevertheless. The private sector can court disaster as an economic strategy as much as the public.

The recession that began in 2008 offers yet another example, in which cheap capital led investors to pour money into real estate beyond any reasonable market demand for it, while lenders pushed subprime mortgages on naive home buyers seeking more house than they often could afford. The economic disaster that resulted from those actions has become amply evident. But it has architectural connections as well, stemming from the overbuilding and overvaluing of residential and commercial real estate that architects were only too happy to design.

Klein's shock doctrine demands a degree of collusion between the public and private sectors, even though that doctrine arises from an incredible polarization between them. Rarely have our politics been so divided between those who see private enterprise as irrationally predatory—a tiger to shoot as Winston Churchill aptly observed—and those who see it, equally irrationally, as the source of all that is good—a cow to milk. This echoes the extreme political philosophies of Karl Marx and Friedrich von Hayek. Both saw freedom as a supreme value, but pursued it in opposite ways, one through the equal distribution of a society's collective wealth by a central government and the other through the equal opportunity to achieve personal wealth with minimal government regulation.

It may be, though, that Churchill's third way—private enterprise as a healthy horse pulling a sturdy wagon—is the only sustainable way forward, and one that professionals such as architects can help create. The professions, by their very nature, balance the public and private, as private enterprises licensed to attend to the public good. Too often, though, professionals do not see themselves as a moderating force between those who want to shoot the tiger and those who want to milk the cow of capitalism. A mistaken view of professional ethics holds that we should do what clients ask of us and remain silent if we disagree with their goals. In fact, we have the opportunity and responsibility to show, through our work and our own example, how to balance private profits and public benefits.

In the example here of the architectural firm redoing the headquarters of a bailed-out bank, the firm has the professional duty to do the work it has been commissioned to perform. The firm also has, however, a professional—and in this case, personal—duty to raise questions about the work's scope and lavishness, given the taxpayer's subsidy of the bank during a severe recession. As professionals, we would all do well to keep Churchill's analogy in mind. Better to be a healthy horse pulling a sturdy wagon, carefully using resources and wisely exhibiting restraint, than to allow ourselves to be shot like a tiger by an outraged public or milked like a cow by a conniving client.

I have never known much good done
by those who affected to trade for the
public good. —Adam Smith

**A**n architect worked for a major retailer, adapting its standard stores to particular locations. The company's merchants insisted on the stores having the most efficient internal layout, with easy access from the adjacent parking lot, although urban communities increasingly wanted the company to adapt its stores to existing commercial areas, with entrances on the sidewalk and parking behind the buildings. While the architect had ideas of how to adapt the store design to these requirements, the company resisted and let it be known that it would avoid communities that would not accept its standard format.

The ethical dilemma here has several layers to it. The architect has been licensed to look after the public good but is working for a company that insists that the good of its profit margins takes precedence over that of the communities in which it builds. The community wants to generate jobs and increase the tax base but also to encourage the public good of having lively streets and active commercial areas. And the company needs the goodwill of the communities in which it operates and the customers on whom it depends but also needs to make a profit and create value for its shareholders. How do we balance public and private goods when they appear to conflict with one another yet are mutually dependent?

Adam Smith rightly warned us not to "affect" or pretend to act on behalf of the public good, without really doing so. The company, for example, could pretend to respond to community demands for more urban-oriented stores by installing fake windows or permanently locked entrances facing the street, giving only the impression of urbanity. Such empty gestures or affectations, as Smith might say, would likely do little to win the community's support. To achieve a public good, we need to act in ways that are actually good for the public, without just feigning to do so.

Smith showed us how, with his paradoxical claim that we can pursue our private interests and still achieve the public good through the workings of the marketplace's "invisible hand." Instead of our affecting "to trade for the public good" as a cover for our pursuit of personal gain, Smith thought that we should accept the inherent selfishness of most people and create a system that harnesses that greed to achieve real public good.

Smith's interest in the public benefit of capitalism often gets lost in the evangelical fervor with which some people insist on their private right to its bounty. The brilliance of the marketplace, in Smith's view, lay not just with its ability to create private wealth but also—and more importantly—with its ability to generate real public good in the process. The rich, said Smith, "are led by an invisible hand...without intending it, without knowing it, [to] advance the interest of the society." The value of the marketplace's invisible hand, in other words, lies in its ability to advance the public good by those with the most personal greed, without their even knowing it.

In this way, capitalism can achieve, by other means, the same ethical goal of most religious ethics. The latter have long held the view that when we help others, we help ourselves; Smith's version of capitalism simply inverts the order in which that occurs: help ourselves and we cannot help but help others. Religions have also challenged the view that we measure wealth according to how much money a person has, something that Smith echoes when he writes that "the beggar...possesses that security which kings are fighting for." The true measure of our wealth, in other words, lies in how many people we help rather than how much profit we make.

In the case of the architect here, trying to balance public and private interests, the more the company responds to people's desire for more adaptable store designs, the better off it will ultimately be in gaining the goodwill of customers as well as community approval. The architect could help the company see that by presenting design alternatives that achieve both the merchants' needs and the communities' demands, knowing that non architects sometimes have a hard time envisioning win-win options until they actually see them. The architect could also use her position inside the company to make the case that the more that businesses help the communities in which they operate, the better everyone does. Smith believed that, and those who have come to believe so fervently in Smith's capitalism need to understand that and believe it too.

# Public Health

**We are caught in an inescapable network of mutuality, tied in a single garment of destiny. Whatever affects one directly, affects all indirectly.** —Martin Luther King Jr.

**An architect working in a large firm noted how often polyvinyl chloride (PVC) was specified for everything from resilient flooring to pipes to windows. She spoke to the firm's lead specifier about the harm PVC causes, and he told her that**

**it was the most cost-effective material in many cases and that the literature from the PVC industry assured him that the material was perfectly safe. She, in turn, pointed him to studies on the toxic effect of PVCs on people and other animals, and suggested less-harmful alternatives. When the specifier would not change the spec, she took the issue to her boss, one of the firm's partners, to decide.**

Immanuel Kant's "duty" ethics provides us with several useful tools when confronted by an ethical dilemma such as this. In his book *Fundamental Principles of the Metaphysics of Morals,* Kant offered this categorical imperative: that we should act as if our actions were to "become a universal law." In other words, we should ask ourselves whether we would want to live in a world in which everyone else acted the same way. We would not want to live in a world in which everyone cheated or harmed others with impunity, and so we should not cheat or harm others, even if some people seem to get away with it, at least initially. Martin Luther King Jr.'s observation that we are all "caught in an inescapable network of mutuality, tied in a single garment of destiny," reinforces Kant's imperative. We may think we can get away with unethical actions, but we never do, since we are inseparably linked to those we harm.

How might that help the partner in this firm decide whether to ban PVC products from the firm's specifications? The marketplace provides an incentive to use this material, which is less expensive than less-harmful materials. Yet the mounting evidence of PVC's potential harm to people and the environment makes a compelling case for banning its use. Kant's duty ethics rests on the idea that we should do the right thing, regardless of its consequences. That is a noble sentiment, although it does not always help us make a decision, since we can never fully separate our decisions from their potential consequences. All action has an aim of some sort, and it can become almost impossible to determine the right action without reference to its intended aim.

But Kant's categorical imperative does offer a useful measure of an action's "rightness." While some might dispute how immediately harmful the use of PVC might be, there is no denying that some of the materials that go into its manufacture, as well as into the product itself, are carcinogenic or have other potentially negative effects on our health. So, if the use of PVC became, as Kant would say, a "universal law" and something that we should all use as much as possible, that is clearly something we would not want to do, any more than we would want any potentially toxic material to be universally employed in as many ways as possible.

In contrast, using a nontoxic substitute for PVC, while possibly more expensive, does pass the "universal law" test. If it is harmless to humans and to other species or ecosystems, then its universal application does not present a problem and we should use it, regardless of the economic consequences of doing so. If it costs more, then we should bear that cost and find other ways to save, and if its use becomes universal, the cost will eventually come down. The partner's decision would seem clear, although an additional duty might justifiably be placed on the architect who raised the issue: to help point the specifier to sources of information about alternatives to PVC. We have, as Kant argued, not only a duty to do the right thing but also a duty to help those affected by those actions. For as King said, "Whatever affects one directly, affects all indirectly," and so with every act of personal responsibility comes an obligation to try to educate others as to why it is their responsibility as well.

## Cultural Differences

A firm received a commission in a conservative Middle Eastern country to design a large project. The most qualified and experienced people in the office available to work on the project were all women, but after the first meeting with the client, the male owner of the firm received a call from the client asking that he put together an all-male project team. The client said he could not work with women and that the community would not accept a project designed and overseen by women.

Islam's holy book, the Koran, has a strong ethical content. It advocates values, for instance, that align with virtue ethics: courage, justice, compassion, forgiveness, responsibility, generosity, humility, and tolerance. At the same time, the Koran argues that we must act in accordance with God's will, even if that conflicts with traditional practices and social customs, reflecting Muhammad's role as a reformer in his own time, using revelation to counter the corruption and conformity that he saw in the society around him. Yet, despite the reformist origin of religions like Islam, when they become enforced social practices, their adherents can resist the very change that prompted the faith in the first place.

Such issues may seem far removed from the architectural profession, but they have become increasingly pertinent as practice has become more global. Architects now often face cultural assumptions and ethical precepts quite different from their own, and deciding how best to deal with those differences becomes an ethical challenge all its own. As is the case here, the difference can seem insurmountable. The widely accepted—although not always widely practiced—equality of men and women in the Western world makes the inequality and the intolerance of women in positions of power in some Islamic cultures seem almost barbaric. What about the Koran's advocacy of justice and responsibility, or its plea for us to see ourselves as equal in the eyes of God, even if that conflicts with tradition or custom? How can such unequal treatment be tolerated in such a devoutly ethical society?

Questions like this may not be of the sort that design practitioners can, or maybe even should, address with clients. It may seem best, in the spirit of the Koran, to approach Islamic society with humility, courage, and forgiveness, accepting its practices as different from our own and trying to work as well as we can within them. From that agnostic position, the firm's partner, upon receiving that call from the client, could have reassigned the women to other projects and put together an exclusively male team. If the firm wanted to produce the very best results it could for its client, then finding the most appropriate way to achieve that within a given culture may make economic sense, even if it conflicts with the Western value of gender equality.

But such pragmatic ethics runs into a paradox. As Karen Armstrong has argued, fundamentalists, whether Muslim, Christian, or Jew, see secular democracy, with its acceptance of difference, as their enemy. "Fundamentalists," she argues, "want to drag religion and/or God from the sidelines to which they've been relegated in modern secular society and bring them back to center stage. And, in this, they've enjoyed considerable success in some ways, though in other ways...it can represent a defeat for religion." Does our acquiescing to the request of a fundamentalist client and culture that we would otherwise find unacceptable make us an accessory to socially enforced inequality? Does the consequence of appearing to employees and peers as an accomplice to intolerance outweigh the consequence of not accepting the client's demand?

This dilemma shows how much global practice requires an even stronger ethical compass than we often need in our own country. While we should show respect for cultural practices different from our own, we nevertheless remain a productive and responsible member of our own environment. We may not have the right to tell another culture what we think is good or bad, but neither do we have the right to leave our own sense of good and bad behind when we practice there. If the firm's partner complies with the client's request, the office could keep the commission but lose the confidence of coworkers and colleagues by engaging in a form of gender discrimination no longer acceptable in the United States. Prophets often became pariahs or outcasts in their own land, but only fools allow themselves to become pariahs by following what they themselves would never profess.

# Obligations to the Client

**Members should serve their clients competently and in a professional manner, and should exercise unprejudiced and unbiased judgment when performing all professional services.**

# Self-Destructive Behavior

**There is no calamity greater than lavish desires.** —Lao-tzu

A client hired an architectural firm to design a large house that he planned to sell quickly for what he thought would be a substantial profit. The architects, in the meantime, had watched the housing market in their area soften and the national housing market drop precipitously. One partner in the firm raised a concern about this with the client and suggested a more modest design that the client could afford and enjoy living in, if he could not sell the house. The client, however, wanted the architects to proceed with the original plan.

We once saw our houses as primarily places in which to live, suited to our needs and meant to be occupied for a lifetime. But houses have also become investments, as much an abstraction as any stock or bond and as much a commodity as anything else intended for trade. This abstraction has contributed to the uniformity and temporality of much mass-produced housing, which most people have accepted as long as housing remained a good investment. The chimera of profit has blinded us to the reality of the poor design and construction of most houses.

The profiteering from housing, of course, became so prevalent that it created an economic bubble that eventually burst, leading not only to massive numbers of foreclosures but also to the collapse of many banks that held the debt from overly leveraged loans and overly optimistic investors. One of the most tangible and essential things in our lives—the roof over our heads—became the basis for such irrational exuberance over so much ephemeral value that we will long look back on this era and wonder how we could have been so oblivious to the risks involved.

Some saw it coming, of course. A number of people who studied the housing market warned of the growing bubble and the consequences of its collapse, but as often happens in periods of feverish financing and rapid asset accumulation, naysayers get ignored. Some architects, at least in private, also remarked at the conspicuous consumption of some clients, who wanted more house than they needed, thinking they could afford it. But doing what the person paying the fees wants has come to trump personal reservations of most professionals, turning us into what philosopher Thomas Hobbes called "artificial persons," in which we set aside our own scruples to serve our clients.

This raises a question about the ethics of service. How much does our duty extend beyond meeting clients' programs to helping them see their wishes in a larger context and their short-term requirements over the long term? Immanuel Kant's duty ethics helps us answer such a question. He would argue that an ethical person—and I would add, an ethical professional—does what is right when viewed in the largest scale and what reason requires, regardless of the possible awkwardness of countering a client's intentions. We should do so not because it might make us feel less artificial but because it serves clients' real interests, whether they see it that way or not.

For clients who request things that may lead to their ruin, the professional has a duty to explain the consequence of that request, the calamity that lavish desires can cause, as Lao-tzu put it. And if clients refuse to listen, we need to be ready to refuse the requests we think ill advised. That can, of course, lead to our dismissal, but this broader sense of service also preserves what it means to be a professional: we should not do for others that which we would not do ourselves.

Not that professionals always get things right. We can make mistakes about the right course to take, especially when the issues involved extend beyond our area of expertise. The client, in the situation described here, may get away with flipping the house and accruing a substantial profit, making the architect's expressed concern about the housing market seem alarmist. But professionals have a duty to speak the truth as we see it, even if ultimately proved wrong, just as we do not have a duty to remain with a client who refuses to listen to our best advice. The lavish desire to keep a commission at all costs can lead to calamity for the professional as well. As Lao-tzu said, "He who knows that enough is enough will always have enough."

# Distrustful Behavior

A client commissioned an architectural firm to design a new building. Although the client had no architectural training, he gave the architects a photo of another building he liked, along with drawings of the plan he wanted. The architects came up with a design that responded to his wishes but that also addressed his needs in ways he had not imagined. The client accepted the architects' recommendations, although he continually questioned the design, nitpicked it during construction, and made disparaging remarks about the architects after the project was done.

Of all the virtues, courage can be the most useful when facing clients who have made up their minds or who think they know what they want before the project assessment and design process even begins. One of the most valuable aspects of hiring an architect, or any professional for that matter, comes from clients hearing not what they want to hear but what they need to hear—what is in their best interest, even if it goes against what they believe to be true. We live in an era, however, in which everyone seems to consider themselves experts, even as the traditional professions face an increasing public skepticism of our judgment and widespread distrust of our expertise. These two trends have some relationship to each other: the more people encounter "professionals" in almost every aspect of their lives, the less they trust professional knowledge.

The devaluing of expertise has led some clients to hire professionals based increasingly on fees rather than on experience or talent, which has forced many professionals to become hyperspecialized in order to set themselves apart in the marketplace for services. While that reflects the increasing complexity of our built environment, the turn to specialization has created a particular problem for architects and designers whose talent lies in seeing something with fresh eyes, imagining possibilities not yet visible to clients, and assessing alternatives not even considered before the design process begins. Arthur Schopenhauer recognized the distrust that often faces those who take leaps of imagination and who discover things that change how we see the world. Most people do not like change or have a hard time seeing something new,

even though most people also know that they need to do so if they are to grow and thrive.

What should architects do when encountering a distrustful or disrespectful client? Some might want to walk away from a commission, and that always needs to be an option in every project if the conditions, financial or ethical, become impossible to work under. Most professionals—and especially most architects and designers who constantly look ahead to the future—begin a relationship with a client optimistically, hopeful that, together, they can create something both powerful and practical. But every professional needs to have enough financial capacity, self-confidence, and courage to terminate a bad relationship with a client. Virtue matters, whether it is the virtue of courage to do what is right or the lack of virtue in others that leads them to do wrong.

But short of walking away, the architects in this situation did the right thing in focusing on what the client really needed, and not just on what he wanted. They found the mean, as Aristotle called it, between being slavishly obedient to the client's initial demands and rashly dismissive of what the client liked, for it often takes more courage to find a middle ground between conflicting views than it does to take one extreme or the other, however much our currently extremist culture sees it otherwise. Persisting in the face of distrust is the sign of the true professional, able to speak the truth despite the client's contrary expectations.

Likewise, it takes courage to maintain one's own self-respect when faced with the distrust of others. In the end, virtue ethics helps us attend to what is most important and most within our own control—our own character—rather than worry about what others may or may not think of us. Knowing that you have done what other professionals would agree is the best job possible under the circumstances is what makes being part of a profession so important. Architects cannot practice without clients, but neither can we let the sometimes uninformed opinions of clients drive our practices. We need to trust others, but even more, we need to trust ourselves.

## Dishonest Behavior

**The art of being wise is the art of knowing what to overlook.** —William James

A university client hired an owner's representative to oversee the architect's work on a major project on campus. The architect involved the owner's representative in all pertinent meetings and correspondence. However, when that representative turned out to be a poor communicator and took many months to convey to the architect the client's decision to make a major change to the building's program, it caused the

# architect to do unnecessary work, expend too much of the fee, and fall behind schedule. The owner's representative blamed the architect and convinced the client of that, forcing the architect to make time-consuming changes to the building design for no additional fee.

Ethical dilemmas can quickly become legal disputes, as in a case such as this, where both the owner and the architect could claim damages because of the lost time and extra work they each endured as a result of poor communication. But ethics can help us understand situations like this in ways that the law may not. The standard architectural contract, for example, barely addresses the need for clients and their representatives to have good communication skills. Nor is poor communication, per se, an ethical violation. But virtue ethics does address the need for honesty and the acceptance of responsibility for actions taken—or in this case not taken—on the part of the owner's representative, or of any party involved in a contractual relationship. By blaming the architects for information that the owner's representative did not convey, the client's team violated a fundamental principle of most ethical codes: that we be honest in our dealings with each other.

Some might call it naive idealism to assume that others will be honest with us; the philosopher William James called it instead the will to believe. Belief in the possibility of a successful outcome, as James observes, remains a major reason for it becoming so, arising out of an expectation of honesty on the part of all involved. When people violate that expectation, they damage not only the relationships on which commerce depends but also their own reputation by betraying that trust. That is where the ethical and the legal can sometimes part ways. In a case like this, the client might appear to have the upper hand, legally: the university has the right to demand that the architect's design meet the requirements of the program for the agreed-upon fee, regardless of who said what to whom and when. Were this to go to court, a judge might insist on adhering to the contractual agreement, however poor the channels of communication between the owner's representative and the architect might have been.

But that legal right may not make ethical sense. The university, in this case, can do untold harm to its reputation by acting in this way, by not accepting blame and by not being honest about who was at fault for the delay. Even if the university won in a court of law, it loses in the court of public and professional opinion, as other architects, some of whom might be alumni and donors, hear of the institution's shoddy treatment of this one firm. Who will trust this client in future projects? Who will want to work for such a client or sign any contract that leaves the firm liable for the poor communication skills of the client's representatives? Ethics, from that perspective, is not naive or idealistic at all. It helps us see what is truly in our best interest, as opposed to what our contracts might allow us to do. Is the university's reputation as an honest, trustworthy client worth losing in order to gain a little more work out of a firm without having to pay an additional fee? Only the most shortsighted institution would agree.

Ethics can also help the architects, in this case, decide how to handle the situation. They, too, might sue the owner's representatives for damages, since it is with them that the real fault for the delay lies. That has its own hazards, however. Apart from whether the architect might win such a suit, it can make other potential clients distrustful of the firm. In a litigious culture such as ours, we have become accustomed to going after what we think is our due, but in a market economy that depends on trust, the best course may involve not seeking a cash award for immediate damages but instead seeing the wisdom, as James said, in overlooking things that, in the long run, may not be in our best interest to pursue. The wisest course here would be for all parties to sit down, without assessing blame, and to figure out how to complete the work as fairly and financially equitably as possible.

## Deceptive Behavior

**When in doubt, tell the truth.**

—Mark Twain

An architect designed a project, at the client's request, to meet the demands of the local community and

**zoning requirements in terms of massing, setbacks, and access. After working with local officials and community leaders to incorporate their concerns into the design, the architect heard the client say that he intended to make some major changes during construction, countering some of what the community had requested. The client also asked the architect to design the project in such a way that these changes could be easily made.**

Modernism made honesty a key virtue. In architecture, that meant that, to be honest, every building should expose its structure and systems and exhibit its materials in an unvarnished manner. The paradox of emphasizing honesty in modern architecture was how rarely it addressed the honesty of clients or practitioners as opposed to the buildings they commissioned or designed. All the talk about expressing how a completed building came to be may have even provided some in the development community and construction industry with a convenient cover for their less-than-honest actions. The honesty of modernism also allowed some owners to demand less expensive or less user-friendly buildings while wrapping themselves in the cloak of virtue.

How should the architect, in this case, deal with the client's deliberate dishonesty toward the community or city officials? Does the architect have an ethical responsibility to meet the clients' needs, even if that means going along with the owner's intention of ignoring the requests of neighbors or regulators? Or does the architect have an equal or greater responsibility to the public, even if that means betraying the confidences of clients intent on betrayal themselves?

Mark Twain's apt aphorism offers some guidance here. The humor of his comment itself involves a bait-and-switch. We expect the beginning of the sentence "when in doubt" to lead in another direction than "tell the truth," yet, upon hearing it, we immediately know the truth of his observation. Deception often occurs among people who should have more doubts than they often do, undoubtedly thinking that they will get away with their lies even when they frequently do not. The client and the architect in this case should both have doubts because of what the community will think of them after they ignore the neighbors' requests. And for that reason, as Twain would say, they both should tell the truth.

Telling the truth, of course, can take many forms. In the case of the architect here, she could start by telling her client that she is uncomfortable with and will not be a part of any effort to alter, intentionally, what she had agreed to do in the building as a result of people's input into its design. She may have doubts as to whether the client will fire her for refusing to go along with his deception, but here again, we encounter Twain's advice. If she has such doubts, all the more reason to tell the truth, since it is the only way that she will know what will happen once the truth is out. She can also tell the community leaders or city officials the truth of her client's intentions. The client might claim that this constitutes a breach of contract by revealing confidential information, but there is no such contractual obligation to withhold information that will harm others or violate the law. Professionals have an obligation to the public good that transcends our obligations to the client's interests, especially when the latter will harm the former.

Just as honesty transformed architecture with the advent of modernism, so too can it transform modern practice. Just as designers help people see what does not yet exist, so too can the design process help clients see the disadvantages of lying, since a future built on lies will eventually harm no one more than the liars themselves. It is just another way to think about honesty in architecture: using design to help people see that, whether in doubt or not, the best policy is to tell the truth.

> **Plenty, indeed, produces cheapness, but cheapness always ends in negligence and depravation.** —Samuel Johnson

 major big-box retailer commissioned an architectural firm to design a new office building on an expansive site near its headquarters in a small city. The client wanted the office to be as efficient as possible and asked the architect to model it after its big-box stores, with the goal of fitting as many employees as possible into the space. While this would put the staff far from any windows, with little visual or acoustical privacy, the client argued that such efficiency fit the image of a discount retailer and that if its store employees could work in a big box, so should its headquarters staff.

The desire of a company to save money or be more efficient seems like a perfectly ethical position to take. After all, public companies have a fiduciary responsibility to their shareholders, who generally want to maximize the return on their investment. At the same time, no one forces employees to work for a company; if they do not like the working conditions—assuming that those conditions meet all health and safety standards—they do not have to seek employment there. That goes for the architects as well. If they do not want to design a big-box office for this client, there are no doubt other firms willing to do so. This has led some to argue for the ethical neutrality of the marketplace, that the economic decisions of people and their relationship to goods and services—again assuming it is all done within the law—have little to do with ethics and mostly to do with rational calculation.

But ethics can help us make those economic calculations in a more holistic and, ultimately, more rational way. Utilitarianism, for example, urges us to not only look at the greatest good for the greatest number but also see our individual good as part of the greater good. Discount retailers should understand that their business model rests on the idea of providing large numbers of people with low-cost goods. Ethics, though, helps us see that the greatest good extends beyond our strictly economic interests. As we have seen when big-box retailers destroy local businesses and then vacate towns for larger, regional stores, the lowest-priced goods can come at a very steep price in terms of their effect on the community's prosperity and well-being. The greatest good, in other words, extends beyond our economic decisions as individuals and includes our overall interests as a group or community.

That broader notion of utility becomes amply evident in the situation described here. Just because inanimate goods, occasional customers, and mobile employees can easily occupy a large, mostly windowless building does not mean that office workers, who sit in one place for eight or more hours a day, can do so. Their productivity, as social science shows, depends partly on their ability to not work in overcrowded conditions, and to see daylight, to have acoustical privacy, and to retain a degree of control over their working environment. And their productivity relates directly to the company's profitability: with the cost of salaries far greater over the life of a facility than the building itself, trying to save some money on bricks and mortar can prove extremely costly in terms of employee happiness and satisfaction, making no sense either economically or ethically. It is one thing to sell low-cost products and quite another to sell short the workers whose dedication and skill are essential to a discount retailer's success.

This highlights the role that architects can play in projects like this. Rather than simply give this corporate client what it thinks is in its best interest, the architect here has an obligation to educate the client about the enormous leverage that small increases of investments in facilities can have on substantial increases in productivity and, with it, the company's profitability. The client might think that the architect just wants a larger fee through a more costly building, and so a part of doing the right thing involves making sure the benefits accrue to as many others as possible. The architect here should offer to do a better building, one that offers workers more light, air, and views, for the same fee, to eliminate the suspicion of featherbedding. Utilitarian ethics ultimately teaches us that we gain more, the more gain we can bring to others.

## Solicitous Behavior

**Your sole contribution to the sum of things is yourself.** —Frank Crane

**n**

**architectural firm that designs a lot of religious buildings had become accustomed to giving money in support of the good works of its clients in the community. But a client of a large, evangelical congregation asked the firm to give to a conservative political cause that the firm's partners did not support. The minister of the church suggested that if the architects did not make a contribution, he would have to rethink his decision to give future commissions to the firm.**

The word *blackmail* has a spatial origin, with links to the landscape. An Anglo-Norse word that originally meant "rent" or "tribute," blackmail referred to the goods that poor farmers paid to freelance guards in exchange for protection from marauders during the border wars between England and Scotland hundreds of years ago. Eventually, blackmail also came to mean the soliciting of payment to withhold incriminating information. That shift in meaning, while subtle, also has significance. Initially, blackmail represented a public way to secure land and possessions during chaotic times, when currency was not available. But the act of blackmail eventually went underground, as an illegal way to extort money to keep something from becoming known.

The AIA's code of ethics prohibits architects from engaging in illegal activities, which includes blackmailing others, but such codes offer much less guidance when others—especially clients who have the power to commission work—exert pressure on us through similarly solicitous behavior. Should the architects, in this situation, keep their political opinions to themselves and donate to the causes their client considers so crucial, or should they refuse to do so and risk losing an important client? Or might they give to both sides of a political campaign, contributing something to the client's candidate and something to another more to their liking?

The reciprocity rule of ethics comes to bear in cases like this. Doing for others what we would want them to do for us also works in the reverse: we should not let others do to us what we would not do to them. If it is unethical for us, as professionals, to pressure clients to give money to a favorite

cause under threat of withholding future work, so too is it unethical for clients to do so to us. This suggests that, rather than acquiesce, refuse, or hedge in their response to the client's threat, the architects should address the real issue with the client, which has nothing to do with politics and everything to do with ethics. If the minister of this church would not want someone to pressure him to support a cause he disagreed with, why should he expect his architects to do so?

The client, of course, might not care or simply say that he has the right to demand such things of those whom he hires. But ethics helps in that case, as well. It provides us with a way to know whom we want to work for and whom we never want to work with again. If clients use their position to assert power over a consultant, then they do not understand the nature of a professional relationship. People should commission architects, as they do lawyers or accountants or doctors, based on their expertise, which they are professionally bound to use to a client's benefit. As Frank Crane observed, our "sole contribution to the sum of things" is ourselves, and that is all a professional can ever contribute—the sum of all that we know and have experienced. By crossing the line to demand that his architects contribute financially to something they personally do not believe in, this client has acted in a profoundly unprofessional way.

What should these architects do? Even if some of them agreed with the client politically, they have a professional—and ethical—duty to refuse to contribute as a firm, although they can do whatever they want personally. And if they lose the commission or never receive another from this client or others like him, the architects should consider themselves lucky. There are many more people in the world who need the services of architects than there are architects able to serve them, and so a client's ethical abuses simply make it easier for architects to know whom to avoid. Let the buyer beware.

## Unrealistic Expectations

**Men in general judge more from appearances than from reality. All men have eyes, but few have the gift of penetration.** —Machiavelli

An architect received a commission from a college that had fired its previous architect for designing a building that was too expensive. The new architect, after discussing the project with the client, saw that the budget was completely inadequate for what the client wanted, and realized that the previous architect, rather than address

**that mismatch, had designed a beautiful building based on what the client had asked for rather than what it could afford. The new architect faced the dilemma of not repeating that mistake with a client whose expectations had not changed.**

In design, as in ethics, there often exists a gap between appearance and reality, between what we desire and the facts of the matter that we may not want to face. That gap takes physical form in the relentless cheapening of almost everything, in which the quality of things diminishes along with their enlargement in size and embellishment of surface. This stems, perhaps, from our almost continual exposure, through advertising, of images of the quality of life that few of us can afford, but all of us are encouraged to want. We have almost come to expect to have more for less, and to expect others to meet that demand or face dismissal. In ethics, such unrealistic expectations lead to the question of where the responsibility for facing facts really lies. Should the holders of such expectations be held responsible for realizing this on their own, or do others have the duty to help them realign unrealizable demands with reality?

The previous architect in this case seemed to have taken the former tack. If the college wanted a building that big, who is the architect to say no?

The responsibility for affording what a client wants lies with the client, not with the designer. As if adhering to Machiavelli's observation that people in general "judge more from appearances than from reality," this architect designed a compellingly beautiful building, whose visual appeal might have inspired the client to do whatever it took to build it. That may seem like a reasonable gamble, but it clearly did not work here, with the client firing the architect for not providing more for less, however much the architect's modern aesthetic represented less-is-more. The new architect would do well not to repeat that error and instead help the client realign expectations with reality. Better to be up-front with a client at the beginning rather than expend a lot of time and energy to achieve the unaffordable or impossible.

This points to a key value of professional service. People should not seek professional help just to have misguided ideas or unrealistic expectations confirmed. We would not visit physicians who did whatever we told them to do, regardless of what truly ailed us, or hire lawyers who argued whatever we instructed them to, regardless of its legal merit. Professionals in every field have a duty to tell clients what they need to hear, whether or not clients want to hear it or decide to follow such counsel. The more the mismatch between our expectations and reality, the more we need honest and unvarnished professional advice, and the better it comes as soon as possible so that we do not languish any longer than necessary under illusion.

Professional duty, of course, does not stop there. The new architect has the duty not only to tell the college what its budget will likely allow but also to show how the college might achieve as much of its original program as possible, making more from less. The often-unrealized promise of modern architecture lies in its potential to maximize multiple uses and minimize space, materials, and expense. This is where design proves itself most valuable: when clients want too much, designers have an obligation to show how just enough is more than anyone would have thought possible. The architect's duty, in that sense, goes beyond telling the truth. It involves giving hope and engaging others in imagining alternatives better than what they originally had in mind. Done well, it should lead not to dismissal but to a process of self-discovery and an enlargement of possibilities that can overcome the most unrealistic expectations. Design offers "the gift of penetration," as Machiavelli put it, and the more we focus on reality rather than appearances, the more we can deploy that gift for good.

*Solve the problem*

## Manipulative Situations

**The greatest achievements of the human mind are generally received with distrust.** —Arthur Schopenhauer

# An architect with a good deal of mass-transit experience in other cities advocated publicly and with

**great ardor for a new light-rail system in his own community, for which most people thought he would likely get the commission. The architect did not see any conflict of interest in his advocacy, since he did not have the commission, and instead argued that his expertise made him the obvious spokesperson for transit supporters in his city. Some thought, though, that his involvement might work against public support because of the apparent self-interest of his actions.**

Much of our politics, economics, and ethics rest on the assumption that people act primarily according to their own self-interest. Politicians often presume that other countries behave on that basis and so form public policies around that belief, while economists take it almost as an article of faith that self-interest guides our financial decisions. Such is the impact Adam Smith's capitalism has had on us. But Smith had a more nuanced view of human behavior than many of his fundamentalist followers might admit. Smith's theory of moral sentiments rested on his conviction that nature endowed us "not only with the desire of being approved of, but with the desire of being what ought to be approved of," of wanting to be what we approve of in others.

Although sounding somewhat convoluted, Smith's theory suggests that people do not act out of self-interest so much as self- and social-approval, and that the concern for what others think of us and of what we think of ourselves is a constraint on selfishness. Moral sentiments do not conflict with economic self-interest so much as complement it. Smith believed that we do better economically when we care about others, about their well-being and their well-wishes for what we do, leading to the paradox at the core of his ethics: the actions most in our self-interest rest with those that most advance the best interests of others.

That paradox also lies at the heart of professional ethics. While professional organizations remain businesses, with profits—when they occur—accruing to the partners or owners, our operations have another primary purpose, the provision of services to clients on behalf of the public good. The most successful firms are ultimately those whose work brings the greatest benefit to others. The architect in this case, advocating for public transit in his community, exemplifies the tension that exists within that equation. His advocacy will help others achieve something of great benefit, even though, in so doing, he will also likely benefit himself if his firm receives the commission to design the system.

That is not guaranteed, especially in public projects that require a competitive process to select consultants, and so his efforts on behalf of the transit proponents could end up being a lot of pro bono work, offered with no commission in return. That is why it matters greatly how professional firms balance selfless and self-interested efforts, knowing that, as Franklin D. Roosevelt observed, too much emphasis on the latter can become the enemy of true affection by other professionals and by the public in return. Smith recognized that, with his admonition that we should care for others' sentiments as a counter to the ultimately self-defeating nature of uncontrolled self-interest.

In this mass transit example, the architect could take himself out of the running for the commission by offering, for instance, to help select the design team should the system get approved. Nothing would do more to win the true affection of others in his community than to make clear his selflessness in supporting something that would benefit the public good without personally profiting from it. This may seem too selfless for some. What if this architect is the best person to design the system? Would not his withdrawing from possible consideration ultimately work against the public's best interest? Perhaps a more balanced approach would be to ensure a fair and fully transparent selection process, so that if his office became a competitor for the commission, no perception of a conflict of interest could occur.

Whichever way the architect here chooses to go, the moral sentiments of the community matter most and should guide his decision. Businesses too often ignore such sentiments or try to manipulate them through marketing and advertising, which Smith would have disparaged as delusional, however apparently successful such strategies might seem in the short run. That especially applies to professional firms, whose real value rests with their reputations. Regardless of how justified we might feel in pursuing our self-interest, responding to the community's sentiment, in the end, makes the most sense.

# Deceiving a Client

Every act of dishonesty has at least two victims: the one we think of as the victim, and the perpetrator as well. Each little dishonesty makes another little rotten spot some-where in the perpetrator's psyche.

—Lesley Conger

A firm with relatively little experience in a particular building type won a commission to the surprise of another, more knowledgeable firm. Later, the latter learned that the winning firm, seeking to boost its credibility in competing for the project, had hired a staff member from another firm, one experienced in projects of this type, and showed the new hire's relevant work as their own in the interview. Although that first firm was credited with the work in small print in the presentation, the firm that won the commission gave

# the impression that they had extensive experience when they did not.

We accept an architectural slight-of-hand if it makes a building appear more pleasing, compelling, or appropriate to its use or context, but we cannot accept deception on the part of architects in pursuit of a commission, however much that deceit may seem justifiable in the minds of those who engage in it. Why do we accept a degree of deception in our physical environment and not among those who design such environments? Lesley Conger offers one answer. Architectural deceit does not have victims; indeed, visual deceptions often happen in buildings in order to avoid subjecting people to something that might disturb or distract them. But deceitful architects do have victims—two in fact: the people deceived and the people doing the deceiving.

Why, then, do so many people deceive others? To even ask the question sounds naive, so entangled has our political and commercial culture become in deception. The growing interest in ethics is itself an indication of how far we have fallen in recent years amidst record numbers of political scandals and puerile Ponzi schemes, all of which victimize not only innocent people, but also the perpetrators of these deceptions, who almost always get caught and so end up being the most deceived of all.

Self-deception certainly applies to the firm in this case, whose partners elided their lack of experience in order to win a commission for which they were singularly unsuited. As so often happens in cases of dishonesty, the perpetrator seems unable to see past the prospect of succeeding with the deception itself, neglecting to think about what would happen if they succeed in their duplicity. For an architectural firm held liable for the performance of the buildings they design, receiving a complex commission that lies beyond its experience level seems like an irresponsibly risky gamble. It is better to be honest and possibly out of work than dishonest and eventually in court facing litigation and liquidated damages.

Ultimately, we are better off economically when we do what is right ethically, despite the apparent short-term gain that deception often seems to offer. That many people in the public and private sector act in unethical ways, creating misperceptions or inaccurate impressions among those whose votes or purchases they want, does not make it smart. Deceivers are usually the most deceived, and they harm not only others, as Conger reminds us, but also themselves.

In the situation here, the firm's lack of experience will eventually become apparent to the client, undermining the confidence and trust so essential to the completion of a successful project. The firm, of course, can hire new staff with the experience necessary to do the work properly, and so lessen the chances of the project imploding, but their fraudulent presentation in pursuit of the commission makes them a victim of another sort, regardless of the outcome. The "little rotten spot somewhere in the perpetrator's psyche," as Conger puts it, has the tendency, like all rot, to grow beyond its initial location. Even if the partners in the firm could care less about their own psychic rot, they cannot control the rotten perception their actions create in the minds of colleagues and co-workers.

Professions play an important role in policing the bad behavior of fellow professionals. This happens formally through codes of ethics and the penalties that come from ethical violations, ranging from collegial censure to loss of licensure, but it occurs informally, sometimes even more effectively, in the loss of respect among peers and the damage to a reputation among potential clients and employees. Professional firms depend upon the ability to attract the best talent and projects, and it can take just one serious deception to make the years to come that much more difficult.

What, then, might this firm have done? Rather than pretend that the work of one new employee counted for experience the firm didn't have, the partners in this case could have partnered with another firm that did have the expertise required to do the project proficiently. That, of course, would have required splitting the fee and sharing the limelight, but it would have been the ethical, as well as the economically and professionally correct course of action, and one that would have prevented that "little rotten spot" from eventually undermining the entire firm.

# 4

# *Obligations to the Profession*

# Members should uphold the integrity and dignity of the profession.

# Greed

First say to yourself what you would
be, and then do what you have to do.
—Epictetus

**A**n architect, working for a design-build contractor, specified a high-end waterproofing material for a basement below the water table to prevent water seepage over time. The contractor, looking for ways to cut costs to increase the profit from the job, wanted to use a much less expensive material that would likely fail prematurely, damaging the building and costing the owner a great deal of money to repair. The architect advised against it, but the head of the design-build firm told her that it was his decision to make and that if she wanted to keep working for the company, she needed to go along with it.

In many ethical conflicts, doing the right thing often has a personal cost. If this architect speaks to the client about the improper substitution of materials, she will expose herself to being fired or at least severely reprimanded by her employer. Yet by not speaking up, she also exposes herself to much worse: to unprofessional behavior in not looking after her client's best interests. She might lose either her job or her reputation.

Not a good choice, but ethics, like design, can help us look at particular situations from different perspectives and at different scales. Seen strictly in terms of short-term benefit, and at a very personal scale, situations like this may lead most people to protect themselves and keep quiet. But from a longer-term or larger perspective—from future users of the building, for example, who will have to deal with the water problems that result from this substitution—the opposite is true: the correct thing to do is to speak up to prevent this from happening before it is too late to fix.

We would reach the same conclusion when we see ourselves in a different time scale. Jobs come and go, employers hire and fire all the time. The only thing we can each control, as the Stoics said, is our own virtue, the quality of our character and the trust that others place in us as a result of it. No one can take that away from us, nor is it anyone else's responsibility except ours. In that light, ethical conflicts such as the one described here are really opportunities for us to employ virtue, to speak the truth in the face of an abuse of power, and ultimately to strengthen the one thing that is truly ours.

That is not to say that there might not be situations in which keeping quiet is the most ethical course. Often an architect will encounter a situation with a client where the two have different preferences about some aspect of a project, such as its furnishing, that involve matters of taste, with no bearing on a building's function or performance. While the architect might have more knowledge to back up a furniture preference, the wisest course involves not making an issue of it and remaining silent about the client's choices. Such exceptions do not invalidate the general rule, however. Being a professional as well as an ethical human being requires that we do the right thing, as best as we can determine it, over doing what is most profitable, expedient, or convenient. And whatever penalty we might pay in the short term as a result, we will always reap more than enough reward in terms of reputation and respect. As the Stoic philosopher Epictetus put it, we need to do what we have to do to be the person we want to be. And what about the apparently negative consequences of doing the right thing—being fired, for instance? Viewed from enough distance, that also has a positive side. However hard it is to see when right in front of us, not having to work for an abusive boss becomes a true blessing.

# Insensitivity

# The sole principal of an architectural firm read books on management with the goal of maximizing the firm's profits and his own income. As a result, he continually restructured the company and redefined his staff's job duties to achieve more efficiency and productivity. Despite all of his efforts at managing the firm well, however, the staff continued to leave for other jobs, and he had a difficult time attracting new employees. Nor did he ever come close to achieving the productivity and profit goals promised by the management books he read.

Managers often think that their primary task involves managing others and achieving the greatest productivity from their staff and profit from their operation. That may be what their job description says and what others expect of them, but it misses the most important and most often overlooked responsibility of managers in an organization: managing themselves. This is much harder than it sounds. With power comes the temptation to use it to control others, and in most organizations this temptation becomes an expectation, since most managers are judged by how well they produce results. Indeed, the more managers push others as well as themselves to the extreme, the more often they are rewarded.

But over the long run, the more managers control their temptation to control others, the more successful they will be. All leaders, by virtue of their standing in an organization, have the strength to master others, as Lao-tzu put it, but very few have the real power that comes from mastering themselves. Ethics has much to offer in that regard. Few people read ethics as a guide to management—although a growing number of business books have made the connection between ethics and economic success—but the history of ethics provides plenty of tips about self-management. This includes virtue ethics's emphasis on self-control, contract ethics's focus on collective cooperation, modern ethics's concentration on good intentions or consequences. In almost every ethical tradition, mastery of the self is an essential aspect of leading a good life.

We have seen, of late, what happens when managers lose sight of that. In pursuit of a life defined in terms of large salaries and lavish lifestyles, the top managers of investment banks fell under the illusion that they could control the extraordinary risks they took with other people's money. If they faced any negative consequences, it came from not pursuing extraordinary profits persistently enough. Self-control in such a climate would have been nothing short of self-destructive. We now know, of course, that such behavior also proved self-delusional, as the under-regulated investment banking industry imploded under the weight of so much uncontrolled greed. It produced what ethicists call "moral hazard," since the banks faced no downside to their irresponsible behavior, having become so big that taxpayers had to bail them out.

At the heart of that financial collapse lay the mistaken idea that mastering others—whether it be their money, their lives, or their livelihoods—can succeed without first mastering ourselves. We think that successful people have the most knowledge, the inside scoop on how things work, but we learn from ethics that truly successful people have the greatest understanding that, as Lao-tzu argued, truth is paradoxical. Success and mastery come only when we succeed at mastering our own desire to succeed at all costs.

That is why the architect here never succeeds as a manager, despite all his efforts. He may know a lot about management theories and techniques, but he had yet to learn to control his own desire to manage others and so ended up treating his employees as if they were objects on an organizational chart rather than people in search of wise leadership. As a result, the more he read about how to increase his staff's productivity, the less success he had in finding and keeping a highly productive staff. Treating others as means to his end, as Immanuel Kant would say, made others want nothing more than to end their relationship with him and to prevent him from mistreating them.

Any success at the expense of others is no success at all. The only real success comes when we help others succeed, even when it comes at our own expense. Were this architect to spend more time listening to the staff about how he might help them achieve their goals, he would find that the productivity of his people and the profitability of his firm would rise as a result. In that light, ethics becomes central to a business's success and essential to leading an organization, reminding us that the most successful managers, above all else, know themselves.

## Jealousy

**Competition brings out the best in products and the worst in people.**
—David Sarnoff

An architect in a large, multidisciplinary firm had led the effort in his state to oppose interior designers becoming licensed, even though one of the designers on his staff had actively supported licensure of her field. The architect publicly insisted that interior designers did not need to be licensed, but privately admitted that he feared architects would lose work to interior designers should they become licensed.

# The interior designer at his firm did not know if she should oppose him or pity him.

Design represents a form of game theory, which looks at how people rationally assess their odds of success in complex or ambiguous situations. When clients commission a designer to create a new product or environment, they do so out of a belief that the benefits outweigh the costs, based on what they think the market will bear or their competitors will do. Likewise, when an architect decides to move in one direction or another with a design, it comes from assessing what the client needs, the designer wants, and competitors might think or do as a result. But in game theory, as in design, it often happens that cooperation wins out over competition. A winner-take-all approach to competition means that we have the most to lose if the other wins, so it is often better to have both sides win something than to possibly be the one who loses everything.

In a design, this sense of cooperation takes many forms: in the way a product feels in our hand, an interior adapts to changing needs, or a building responds to the city around it. No design succeeds despite everything else. If the act of designing has characteristics of play—of imagination, speculation, and experimentation—so too does design follow gamelike rules, in which some degree of cooperation and coordination must occur if it is to work at all. But even the best players have their blind spots, as is the case here with architects and interior designers battling over whether the latter

should be licensed. As David Sarnoff observed, competition may lead to better products, but it seems to bring out the worst in people, which is certainly true in the competition over licensure.

Interior designers argue that their field deserves licensure because, like architecture, it involves people's health, safety, and welfare. Bad interior design can make it hard for people to find the exits in a fire, or harm people with the outgassing of materials, or inhibit their ability to work because of too much noise or too little privacy. We all spend most of our lives inside buildings, and so it seems worthwhile to ensure the safety of these interiors by regulating those who design them. Architects, in contrast, argue that they, as the designers of the entire building, have legal responsibility for the interior as well as the exterior, and that licensing interior designers will prevent architects from overseeing all aspects of the architecture to ensure that it works together seamlessly. Because of the complexity of buildings, it also seems logical that a single source be responsible for coordinating all parts.

The game here appears to be zero-sum: if one side wins, the other loses. But both architects and interior designers know that almost nothing is entirely a zero-sum proposition, and the licensure battle proves that. With each side battling the other for so many years in so many states, both end up looking bad. Architects seem paranoid about the "real" intentions of interior designers, who in turn seem envious of what architects have, while both appear almost desperate to gain at the expense of the other. As we know from the "prisoner's dilemma" in game theory, the two prisoners realize, after being tempted to pin the crime on their compatriot, that cooperating with the authorities and confessing leads to the best outcome for both. Ethically, that entails each setting aside the desire to win at the expense of others—and likely losing as a result—to find a way that all win to some extent, with everyone coming out farther ahead.

Applied to the licensure battle between architects and interior designers, that ethic—at the heart of all design activity—should lead them in a very different direction than the one they have pursued. Both sides need to focus on what matters most to the other and then find a solution that addresses those concerns as much as possible with the fewest disadvantages to each. Maybe the best way to do this involves turning it into a design process, pairing architects with interior designers and letting them cooperate in exploring possible alternatives, with a national competition to recognize and implement the best ideas. Design becomes most valuable when finding win-win solutions to seemingly no-win situations like this, and we would go a long way toward demonstrating the value of what we do by showing how well our process works when applied to ourselves.

## Betrayal

They talk of a man betraying his country, his friends, his sweetheart. There must be a moral bond first. All a man can betray is his conscience.

—Joseph Conrad

An architect, commissioned to design a church, was the last of three firms to interview for the project. During the

**interview, the church committee asked the architect some questions based on what her competitors interviewed just before her had said about her firm and its work, and about the low fee that they thought any firm winning the commission should charge. She corrected the misperception of her firm and also told the client that such a low fee would make it impossible for any architect to do a credible job, all the while wondering why the other architects had said such things in an interview.**

Words can guide us in some of the most troubling ethical dilemmas. "Betrayal" is one such word. It has a lot of synonyms, some involving the betrayal of a relationship (disloyalty, unfaithfulness, infidelity), some the betrayal of trust (treachery, duplicity, perfidy), and some the betrayal of truth (dishonesty, deception, deceit). The sheer number of words we use to describe betrayal seems to show how often it happens, and in how many different ways people can disappoint, undermine, fool, or backstab each other. These aspects of human behavior that most embarrass us often accrue the

greatest number of words or euphemisms, as if we use language as some sort of salve to lessen the pain that we bring on ourselves.

Religion helps us deal with betrayal, which makes the case described here all the more troubling. Not only did this architect's competitors (and colleagues) appear to undermine her through what they said about her, but the client—a church—repeated the falsehood and at least appeared to believe it. As so often happens in human affairs, those qualities of character that we most fear in others sometimes reveal those that we most fear in ourselves. Betrayal may be one of the most dreaded acts, but if our language is any guide, it is also one of the dreads most often acted out.

While it might not have been obvious to this architect, confronted in the interview with her peers' underhanded statements, betrayal is not always what it seems at first. As the novelist Joseph Conrad observed, when people betray others, they actually betray themselves. The firm that undermined their competitor in front of a potential client could not have done a better job to ensure that they would not get the job: they betrayed their lack of decency and integrity, and lack of professionalism and collegiality, reinforcing the rightness of the client's decision not to hire them.

At the same time, the architect who was betrayed, by being honest in her response to the client's challenge, by refusing to undermine her colleagues in return, and by remaining true to what it means to be a professional when others have forgotten how, did much to secure the commission. She revealed to the client what kind of person she was when treated unfairly, demonstrating a strength of character that no doubt serves her well in the sometimes unseemly world of construction.

The client betrayed something else. In conveying to the architect what the other firms had said, the interviewers revealed their own insecurity and inexperience in such matters. While they did not initiate the falsehood, they communicated it and kept it going, without thinking that what one competitor says about another might not be fair or even true. If the competing firm, in an act of treachery and duplicity, knowingly betrayed her, the client unknowingly betrayed her by believing—or at least pretending to believe—their lies.

Utilitarian ethics argues that we should attend to the consequences of actions, without regard to the intentions behind them. Even though the church group may not have intended to lie in conveying what the previous firm had intentionally and falsely said about the architect, the consequences were much the same and thus equally unethical. While this architect might want to file a complaint against the firm that lied about her, she also might want to remain wary of a client so open to the betrayal of others. Such are among the reasons why we build places of worship to begin with: to help us learn how to recognize duplicity and deception and to take none of it on faith.

# Treachery

An out-of-town architectural firm teamed up with a local firm to design a new building for a public university. The faculty worked well with the firms, who designed a modern building that nevertheless matched the massing and materials of the other buildings on campus. The president of the university, however, wanted a more traditional building, with columns in front, and he asked the local firm to redesign the building's exterior without telling either the faculty or the out-of-town firm, presenting the redesign to the board of trustees, who quickly approved it. The local firm, originally hired to design the building, now had to decide what to do.

The association of a local architectural firm with an out-of-town one can work well if both trust each other and respect what each brings to a project. The outside firm typically has experience in a particular building type or standing as expert designers, while the local firm often brings to the partnership knowledge of the regulations and requirements of its region. But, like any arranged marriage, such associations can go sour. The out-of-town firm can spend so much of the fee on the design that it leaves too little money for the local firm to oversee the work needed to get the structure built. Or, as happened in this case, the local firm can use its proximity to and familiarity with the situation to its advantage, undermining its associates and positioning itself as the client's primary advocate.

Treachery like that succeeds only if allowed by those who have the power to stop it. The university's president, in this case, initiated it by stepping in and commandeering the project, without informing the faculty and staff who had worked with the architects on the building. The president might have the authority to do so, but at what cost to his colleagues' confidence in him as a leader? By undermining the project's design team, he ended up undermining himself in the eyes of everyone involved, including those who went along with his double-dealing. As Benjamin Franklin observed, treachery makes the treacherous look like fools, without the wits—or self-assurance—to be honest.

The local architects faced the dilemma of following the president's request or taking responsibility for being part of a team of professionals. By siding with the president and redesigning the project without telling their colleagues, the local architects benefited financially, as they finished the project for the university, but at the cost of their firm's reputation. As the old Irish saying puts it, "treachery returns," and it does so in ways that no one can predict. What other firms will want to work with this one, knowing how its architects have undermined their colleagues in the past? What other clients will trust them to do what is right in the face of political pressures? And when will they, too, become the victims of the treachery they once employed, returning to them in spades?

Ethics is a lot like lifecycle costing in a building. As architects know, what may seem like a smart financial move by a client to choose the lowest bid or cheapest product can, over time, prove costly as failures mount, and repair and replacement costs accrue. Lifecycle costing looks at the real costs over time, often finding that somewhat higher initial costs more than pay for themselves over the long run. Consequence-focused ethics does the same. It asks that we look at the full results of our actions over time to assess their real costs to us and to others, and it helps us avoid making what may be the most expedient choice at the moment for which we will pay dearly in the end.

The best course, as Franklin suggests, is honesty. The president should have been honest with his faculty and his architects, and the associate firm should have been honest with its out-of-town colleagues about the president's feelings. Without the wits to be honest, the university and the local firm simply made themselves look foolish. The outside firm could quietly accept the bastardizing of its design, but it, too, could also choose honesty, taking its name off of a building that no longer represented its best work and letting others know of what happened with that client and the other firm. Treachery may not always return directly as more treachery, but it always returns as damaged reputation, which in the professional world is what ultimately makes the difference between success and failure.

## Unfairness

**Don't undertake a project unless it is manifestly important and nearly impossible.** —Edwin Land

**An American architectural firm working in China discovered that it must compete with offices that exist in the Chinese architectural schools, run by faculty with students providing nearly free labor. These in-school offices had lower fees and a much larger staff than any private firm could provide, making for unfair competition. The clients, however, said that this was a common practice in**

# their country and seemed pleased by the downward pressure it brought to the cost of professional services. The American firm had to decide if it wanted to continue to compete under such circumstances.

One challenge of the global economy lies in the fact that different nations have different laws, expectations, and ways of working, some of which may seem unethical to those not accustomed to them. What is unfair competition in one country may be appropriate and affirming in another, as in the case described here. The United States has labor laws that prohibit using students as unpaid workers on fee-paying projects, not only because of the possible exploitation of a vulnerable population but also because it gives those who have access to student labor a perceived unfair advantage over those who pay all of their employees. But in a country like China, where such school-based offices exist, they represent a way to give students real-world experience and a way for schools to help with local development efforts. One culture's conflict of interest may be another's confirmation of community.

The firm trying to compete in such a situation has a couple of decisions it must make. First, it must decide how much it wants or needs to compete for work in such a place. As inventor Edwin Land put it, the decision gets down to how manifestly important and nearly impossiblxe the work

might be. If not important or without challenge, the work may not be worth the effort, especially if the deck seems too stacked against the firm. But if important or challenging enough for the firm to want to pursue, the work prompts a second decision: should the firm accept the terms of the competition or make an effort to change them? The firm could, for example, try to join forces with the most competitive of the school-based offices, thus offering the client the advantages of both professional and educational participation in the project. Or it could try to convince the client to not let the school-based offices compete for work, pointing out the unfair advantage those offices have over firms with paid staff.

Such decisions highlight a larger dilemma at the heart of professional practice. While professions operate small businesses that must meet payroll, cover overhead, and pay the rent, the professions also have an ethical obligation to further knowledge in the field and prepare students for leadership roles. Indeed, many practitioners teach in professional schools, blurring the boundaries between work and education. In the case of in-school offices, that blurring may seem to cross the line, going beyond the educating of students about practice to the developing of a practice that uses students under the guise of education. Still, it becomes difficult for a professional firm to protest the use of students in any competitive situation, since many private offices use interns and often pay them salaries considerably lower than what year-round, full-time staff receive. Where, then, do we draw the line between a private office full of interns and a school-based firm full of internlike students?

The ethics here may rest less on perceived conflict of interest, which may vary considerably from one culture to another, and more on our duty to focus on the best solution for the client, whoever ends up winning the commission. As Land also said, "Every creative act is a sudden cessation of stupidity," and so should every professional firm see a competitive situation as just such a creative opportunity. From that perspective, the firm here could see the "unfair" competition of the school-based offices as an important and nearly impossible challenge, which makes it ripe for the imaginative leap that constitutes the creative act at its best. Instead of walking away from or complaining about the competitors, the firm could see the situation as a chance to excel, even in the face of daunting odds, with creative ideas that look at the clients' needs more broadly and unexpectedly. That is what design does best and how the best design can succeed despite even the most unfair competition.

## Uncertainty

**The more enlightened our houses are, the more their walls ooze ghosts.** —Italo Calvino

# An architect, asked to evaluate a public school for possible conversion into a charter school, heard the janitor talk

**about the ghosts in the building. The janitor claimed that several people had seen the ghosts and that one ghost in particular sometimes toppled things or threw boxes in his way, although the apparitions mostly minded their own business. When others in the school confirmed the janitor's story, the architect wondered if he should tell the charter-school client about it, since the building otherwise served the client's needs very well.**

Professions generally define themselves based on their knowledge of some measurable aspect of the world. Physicians know about bodies, architects about buildings. With that self-conception, professionals sometimes have a difficult time dealing with what we don't know or cannot measure. We see this in medicine with the difficulty Western culture has had relating the mind and body, the unpredictability of the one and the (relative) predictability of the other. Likewise in architecture, we can have a hard time explaining the inexplicable aspects of a place, whether it be the "quality without a name," as the architect Christopher Alexander puts it, or the ghosts that some see in buildings, as in the situation here.

The ethical issue is not about the immeasurable or unseen character of things; that lies in the realm of metaphysics. The ethics involves what we do with such knowledge. Do we have the duty to tell all that we have seen and heard, or do we have a responsibility to remain quiet about what we have not seen or cannot prove? Kant's ethics argues that we should tell the truth as we know it, regardless of the consequences. From that perspective, architects have a professional duty to tell a client about all aspects of a building and not withhold any information that might affect a client positively or negatively. The janitor's ghost story might frighten the client or ruin the chances of the client buying an otherwise perfect building. But, as Kant might say, we should do our duty and let the chips fall where they may.

But do we have the duty to perpetuate a possible phantom of someone's imagination? Can too rigid a view of honesty lead to dishonest or delusional results? Such questions lead to a more nuanced view of honesty, one in which we distinguish between what we know for sure as part of our area of expertise and what we do not know for sure but feel obligated to disclose nevertheless. Professional knowledge focuses on certainty, on what we can prove or what the majority of our peers consider true. We may justifiably fear that any admission of uncertainty or a lack of knowledge might increase our liability and might tempt us to avoid talking about anything that we cannot say for certain. But, as Calvino suggests, the more-enlightened professional, like the more-enlightened house, "oozes ghosts," acknowledging that there remains much that we do not know, cannot tell, or may never understand about the world in which we live.

Professionalism, in other words, demands a degree of humility and enough confidence to admit to the limits of professional knowledge. In the case of the ghosts in the school building, the architect needs to tell the client about what the janitor said. The architect does not have to believe the tale or advise the client what to believe about it, but it remains information that the professional needs to divulge, for what it's worth. That ethical obligation has an ironic result. Rather than represent weakness on the architect's part, the admission of things about which we do not know will make him more human in the client's eyes as well as more of a professional, a person who knows the limits of his knowledge as well as the responsibilities of his field.

The real danger lies in not knowing the limits of our knowledge. The philosopher Gilbert Ryle argued that when we make up terms to describe some phenomena we do not understand, it can lead us to believe that, because we now have a word for it, what may be nothing actually exists. That we have a word like "ghost" does not mean ghosts exist. But such ghost words do remain a useful reminder that we do not and may never understand aspects of our experience. Better to admit the existence of what we cannot explain than to be haunted by the specter of overconfidence.

# Cheating

> In our society, art has become something that is only related to objects, and not to individuals, or to life.
> —Michel Foucault

An intern hears about a website that contains the questions on the licensing exam, posted by people who have already taken the electronic test. She knows that she could look at the website without anyone knowing and that some of her friends in the same situation have already perused the site, giving them an advantage. At the same time, she knows from her years of education and her upbringing that cheating on examinations is wrong and ultimately self-defeating.

Cheating remains among the most obvious ethical violations. Whether it involves peeking over the shoulder of a classmate during a test or plagiarizing text from a website, cheating has long been prohibited in schools and a cause for a failing grade if caught. This stems from the fact that cheaters mainly cheat themselves by not taking the time to learn the material and by thinking that they can get ahead without putting in the required effort. The world does not work that way. In the end, it rewards those who have expertise and the experience that comes with hard work while eventually weeding out the cheaters and frauds.

Without the close attention the academy pays to cheating, and with the greater potential for cheating that the availability and anonymity of the internet provides, those preparing to take licensing exams have a greater degree of freedom than ever before. We all now have access, via the web, to amounts and types of information never before possible, which threatens the disciplines that professions help oversee as well as the very idea of discipline itself. Michel Foucault's ethics offers some useful insight here.

Foucault showed how subjectivity had arisen in concert with the disciplinary structures of modern culture—our schools, governments, and professions—and how those same structures punished those who did not fit or who consciously rebelled against the alliance of individualism and the state. To liberate ourselves from what each of us has become in what Foucault characterized as our highly disciplined, moralistic modern era, he urged us to embrace what he called the "aesthetics of existence," in which each of us continually reimagines ourselves and our conception of a good life. Architects constantly conceive of new ways to live and new forms of a good life through the environments we create. As the philosopher Timothy O'Leary has argued, Foucault saw "the art of ethics" as a creative activity open to possibilities and open to all simply by our being alive.

Foucault's ethics seems particularly pertinent to architects, who give form to life in everything we design, and also especially ironic, since our field has embraced the very subjectivity and discipline that Foucault saw as a barrier to our creating our own conception of a good life. Thus the architectural field recognizes and awards highly individualistic, "star" designers, whose young admirers often imitate the form of their work with little critical examination of the life implicit in their architecture. At the same time, the field enforces the codes, information, and requirements necessary to practice as an architect, licensing those who can demonstrate a command of that knowledge, with little credence given to those who question the assumptions that led to those regulations in the first place.

That brings us back to the question of cheating on a licensing exam. Whether by sharing questions on the internet after taking the test or by studying them online before doing so, such cheating is wrong because the only person we cheat is our ourselves and the only existence we shortchange is our own. Also, the organization responsible for preparing the licensing exam must now spend a lot of money to create new questions, showing how we all pay for the dishonesty of a few through higher costs and potentially higher fees to cover replacing the test.

But we pay an ethical as well as a financial price for this. If each of us has the opportunity to construct a meaningful life for ourselves, to create our own aesthetics of existence, as Foucault said, based on what we see as a good life, then cheating signals our failure to do so. It is not just that we deceive those grading the exam as to how much we know, but also—and more importantly—that we deceive ourselves as to who we are and what we are doing. The punishment for such cheating may not be externally enforced, as often happens in school, but it will be personal and existential, something none of the cheaters can ever escape or excuse. At the same time, cheating on an architectural licensing exam misses the point of being a licensed architect. Architects do not just make artful objects but, as Foucault reminds us, we also play a role helping others see their lives aesthetically, as works of art capable of amazing beauty and imagination. None of us, architects included, can cheat our way there.

# Chapter

# 5

# *Obligations to Colleagues*

Members should respect
the rights and acknowledge
the professional aspirations
and contributions of their
colleagues.

# Office Affairs

> Love, by reason of its passion, destroys the in-between, which relates us to and separates us from others. —Hannah Arendt

The married owner of an architectural firm had carried on a long-term love affair with one of his unmarried employees. No one ever talked about it openly in the office, and the owner didn't seem to show overt favoritism toward his mistress, although the relationship between the two made other staff members uncomfortable, especially at office events that included his spouse. Some employees thought that they should confront the owner about the affair, while others thought that it was none of their business.

Work life and love life rarely mix, even though a long tradition of doing so exists in architecture. This may stem partly from the profession's extraordinary time demands and perhaps from the widespread desire of many architects to integrate work and life. Much of what we design seeks to integrate people's lives with the environments we envision for them, and it seems natural to want to achieve a similar kind of integration in our own lives, as the number of partnerships between spouses in architecture shows.

Ethical dilemmas arise, however, when, as Hannah Arendt put it, doing what we love "destroys the in-between," the space that both connects and separates us from others. In the case of the owner–employee love affair, it collapses the necessary distance that we maintain at work with our coworkers and colleagues, however friendly we might be in the office or even after hours. Ethics requires such distance. It asks that we look dispassionately at a situation and consider what is the right thing to do for all involved, however much it may go against our own perceived interest.

When a boss destroys the in-between that ensures a degree of fairness and equity in an office, it puts everyone at risk. That risk extends not just to the staff members, who recognize the unfair advantage of one of them, but also to the employee engaged in the affair, whose job security has come to depend as much on the boss's affections as on the quality of her work, and to the firm's owner, whose leadership depends on his workers' dedication. The very integration that he may seek through love of another can lead to the complete disintegration of what he and others in the office most love.

The ethical dilemma also extends to the owner's spouse. She has the most to lose from her husband's affair, and everyone in the office knows it, which makes the entire staff undeservedly complicit in the boss's unethical behavior toward his own wife. While it is often best to stay out of others' affairs-of-the-heart, it is also unfair of the boss to expect his employees to keep a secret they should not have to keep. They may not have an obligation to tell the spouse about the situation in the office, but they do have a responsibility to convey to their boss their discomfort with it.

No one wants to broach a subject like this with the person who holds the purse strings and makes employment decisions, so it may seem easier to stay silent or to leave as soon as another job opportunity arises. But this leads to what in ethics is known as the "problem of dirty hands," in which we must choose between alternatives, all undesirable. This problem often gets applied to political leaders who find themselves caught among mutually exclusive choices and must decide on the lesser of evils, but we all get our hands dirty when we enter an ethical fray. Employees in the case here have dirty hands whether they remain silent or speak out about the situation, and so, from an ethical perspective, it is better to come clean than to keep our hands in the dirt and our heads in the sand.

To maintain the "in-between" with their employer, the employees might let their boss know of their concerns indirectly and even anonymously, through an unsigned letter, to reduce the possibility of him shooting the messenger. But ethics demands that something be said. If we are to have dirty hands, better that it comes from doing what we think is right than from participating in what we know to be wrong.

## Working Hours

Anyone can do any amount of work, provided it isn't the work he is supposed to be doing. —Robert Benchley

The principal of a large architectural firm also taught at a nearby university, which took up much of his time during the week. He expected his staff to be there working while he was at school, but the principal also wanted his staff in the office on weekends, always on Saturday and often on Sunday, when he was there. While he paid his people well, he did not pay overtime to his salaried

# staff members, who claimed that they worked for less than the minimum wage given the number of hours they put in at the office. Several of the employees experienced marital problems because of the long hours and had to decide whether they could continue working there.

Part of being a professional involves working long hours or, rather, the number of hours it takes to do a professional job with the task at hand. As a result, salaried professionals often end up spending more time at work than hourly coworkers, ideally not just out of a feeling of obligation to employers, colleagues, and careers but also out of a sense of dedication to the quality of the work. That becomes even more pronounced in a profession like architecture, in which the open-ended creative process can take longer and have fewer definitive end points than other, more quantifiable fields.

Still, a difference remains between doing the work we do out of a commitment to our craft and what we do because of a boss's unreasonable demands. Just because an employer works in unhealthy ways does not mean that others in an office must follow suit, however much their jobs may depend on it. Every professional will have many projects and possibly even many jobs with different employers over a career, but every professional also has but one career, one calling, and our care and cultivation of that matters more than the peculiarities of the particular person signing our paychecks. If a job so interferes with our real work that we no longer have the time or energy to pursue the purpose that underlies our being professionals in the first place, then the job must go, however inconvenient the loss of an income may be over the short run.

Robert Benchley made light of this in his observation that people will do any amount of work if it is meaningful to them, and by implication, as little work as possible if it is not. Benchley's humor, though, reveals the paradox that underlies our notion of the work ethic. That ethic arose in the West, as Max Weber argued, out of a belief among some Protestant denominations that financial prosperity was a sign of God's blessing, and hard work a road to salvation. That view, however, turned work into an end itself, overlooking the larger purpose behind the work, apart from paying for the things we need to keep working. In architecture, like any of the arts, that paradox can take a somewhat different form. We might enjoy the work more because of its creative aspect, but it often still remains an end in itself, preventing us from having the time to enjoy much else in life, as is the case here of the workaholic principal and his staff.

If he is to avoid losing his employees, the principal of this firm needs to see the work ethic differently. He should do what he can to help his employees find meaning in their work, by giving them responsibility, encouraging their innovations, and supporting their decisions. The more often work involves doing what we would do anyway, whether paid or not, the more it becomes something that we look forward to devoting our time and attention to. At the same time, the principal should reevaluate his own work life. Even if he enjoys both his academic and professional duties, working all the time destroys all enjoyment in work. That, in turn, suggests a new kind of work ethic, one that is not about the quantity of work but its quality. What the principal should care about is the work itself: is it any good? And once we put quality above quantity, we realize that the best way to do good work is to have a good life, one that keeps things in balance, and to be a good example for others trying to do the same in theirs.

## Labor Law Violations

Do something for somebody every day for which you do not get paid.
—Albert Schweitzer

A recent graduate of an architecture school wanted to work for a well-known architect whose work she admired. She sent in her resume and a few

**samples of her work, and the architect's assistant called her to come in for an interview, during which she was offered a position in the firm without pay. When she hesitated, the assistant said that many recent graduates like her wanted to work there and that if she did not take the offer, plenty of others would. She was not independently wealthy and would have to borrow money or take a second job to meet her expenses, but she wondered if the experience working for the architect would be worth the price.**

Nonprofit organizations and even some government positions have a tradition of offering unpaid internships to students and recent graduates eager to learn on the job. But for-profit businesses, such as an architectural firm, must obey labor laws, including paying at least the minimum wage, or face financial penalties and potentially even jail. Not all architects have seen things this way. Some, such as Frank Lloyd Wright, not only had employees pay him to work in his office but also had them working on his farm as well as in his drafting room, justified as an educational experience. More recently, a few well-known architects have taken advantage of the number of students and recent graduates eager to work for them by allowing them to work without pay, again, often justifying it as an extension of their education.

Peer pressure and the threat of lawsuits have largely ended such exploitation, but this practice revealed the confusion that sometimes occurs in a creative field like architecture, between a profession and an art. If arts organizations can have unpaid interns, why not an art-oriented architectural firm? The problem with that argument is that it conflates nonprofit and for-profit entities and glosses over the unfair competition that this creates for a private firm. It is unfair not only to the workers who must find other funds to support themselves but also to competing firms who do pay their employees. Some poorly managed architectural firms may not be making much profit, but they still compete in a for-profit world and so must follow labor laws, however much paying even a minimum wage to one's staff may cut into whatever profits do exist.

Another source of the confusion comes from the aristocratic sensibility of some architects, whose behavior echoes the arguments of another aristocrat, Aristotle, who thought that paid work somehow degrades the mind. Architecture once represented one of the respectable activities of noblemen, and that sense that we should engage in this work out of love, rather than money, remains a relatively common, and for some, an appealing aspect of this field. But architecture has become not just an amateur sport, something to pursue purely for the love of it, but also a professional activity, responsible for shaping the buildings and environments in which we spend most of our lives and for protecting the health, safety, and welfare of the people who use what we design. Architects may love their work, and like artists, spend long hours at it, but that love should be freely given and not required of employment. Foolish architects violate labor law and endanger their practices just to save on salaries; wise ones pay employees well and then inspire them to devote their hearts and souls to their work, receiving far more reward for the investment.

So what should you do when offered a job without pay? Virtues such as honesty, courage, and a sense of justice come in handy in such situations. While exploitative employers may not listen, you should speak the truth and remind them that they are violating labor law, endangering the firm with severe penalties, and unfairly competing with other firms that do compensate their staff. If that seems unlikely to have any effect, you might try a creative compromise. Taking a cue from Albert Schweitzer's admonition that we all do something pro bono every day, you might offer to work for free on pro bono projects that you will help the firm find, thus enabling you to get the experience you want in the firm, helping the firm stay within the law by having its unpaid staff work on truly nonprofit work, and most of all, aiding the many people and communities in need of design services for which they themselves cannot pay. The firm that accepts that counteroffer is the one you want to work for.

# Crediting Coworkers

**A**n architect working in a firm did most of the design and management of a project, but upon the completion of the project and the subsequent press that it received, the firm's principal took all of the credit, as if he had done the work, and never acknowledged his staff or the architect who had, in fact, been most responsible for it. When the architect asked her boss if she could be credited for the work, he told her that she can take all the credit when she had her own firm, but it was his right to do so as the owner of this one.

Architecture remains one of the most complex and collaborative of all the arts. It demands a lot of people to make it happen, not just in architectural firms but also among the many consultants and contractors who help create, calculate, and construct buildings. In such a collaborative enterprise, the giving of proper credit becomes one of the most common and confusing areas of ethical conflict. Everyone involved in a project deserves acknowledgment, yet the numbers of people involved can be in the hundreds, if we include everyone. How do we meet our duty to credit the people most responsible for a project within the limits that press releases, public talks, and print publications put on us?

Immanuel Kant's ethics offers one measure of our duty in such situations. He urged us to see all others, whatever our relationship to them might be, as ends in themselves rather than means to our own ends. At first glance, that may not seem to offer much guidance. How do we define means and ends in the case of crediting those involved in the creation of buildings? Is not everything and everyone engaged in design and construction a means to the end of getting a building built that meets people's needs within the budget and schedule? Certainly the focus in the architectural media on the completed structure, with little attention paid to the process of its creation, reinforces this bias of seeing buildings as the end, whatever the means used in the making.

Kant's advice does have value in cases like this, however. The principal of this firm may have the legal right to claim responsibility for this project, having "stamped" the drawings and so accepting the liability should something go wrong. But ethically, according to Kant's prescription, he does not have the right to claim sole responsibility for something that others did. His employment of others does not give him the right to use them as means to his end; rather, he owes them the credit they are due as much as possible, knowing that in some cases, such as a newspaper report, long lists of acknowledgments may not be practical. What matters, as Kant would say, is the intention to give proper credit, even if it does not always happen because of space or time limitations in the media.

The principal of this firm would still be within his legal right to take full credit if he wants, and this is where Wittgenstein's observation becomes relevant. If knowledge is based on acknowledgment—if knowing involves also knowing whom we are indebted to for what we know—then the principal's lack of acknowledgment represents a kind of ignorance on his part. That ignorance can take many forms. Not crediting employees is the fastest way to lose them and, with that, their skills and experience, the very things the firm's principal claims as his own.

It also reveals the principal's lack of confidence in his need to claim what is not his, undermining his authority among the other employees as well as among clients who also know who really did the work on their projects. By not acknowledging others, the principal disempowers himself and damages his firm, which is no doubt the opposite of his intention. By treating others as a means to his ends, he ultimately ends up without the means to treat others this way again. And those who acknowledge the self-destructive nature of this principal's behavior end up having the knowledge to understand the situation and never repeat his mistake. Only through full disclosure can we bring real closure to any architectural project.

> Human diversity makes tolerance
> more than a virtue; it makes it a
> requirement for survival. —René Dubos

A firm seeking to fill a position had more than its share of excellent applicants, one of whom was disabled and would require that some changes be made to the office, in terms of wheelchair access, restroom design, and the like. Some of the firm's partners argued that they had enough other good candidates that they did not need to go through the expense of making physical changes to their office to hire a disabled employee, while a few others thought that they needed to make the office handicapped accessible anyway and that this hire would give them a good reason to do so.

The Americans with Disabilities Act, signed into law in 1990, has transformed how employers accommodate employees' physical needs by making access for the disabled a civil right as much as a building code requirement. It has become, in other words, an ethical and legal issue as much as an architectural and technical one, based on the universal right of all people to have access to buildings and the spaces in and around them. That universal right has led, in turn, to universal design, in which the removal of architectural barriers benefits not only the relatively few people who have permanent disabilities but also all who, at various times in life, have limitations in mobility, whether as a parent with a stroller, an adult on crutches, or an elder with a walker.

The very basis of ethics, argued the philosopher Emmanuel Levinas, lies in our taking responsibility for others out of a realization of how we are both separate and inseparable from them. The more we recognize and respect the diversity of others, the more we see and accept it in ourselves, in our own being. Such an embrace of diversity is not just virtuous, something that we should do because reason tells us that it is good to do so, but also, as the biologist René Dubos suggested, it is "a requirement for survival," a requirement made visible in universal design. In accommodating people with various abilities, universal design ensures that all of us, whatever our capacities, have equal access to the designed environment and an equal chance of surviving—and thriving—in it.

The question of whether this firm should hire and physically accommodate a disabled person is not the real question to ask. We are all differently abled, each in our own way and at various points in our lives, and so making a space handicapped accessible really involves making it accessible to everyone, including ourselves and everyone else. The litigation that can arise as a result of not doing so is, thus, not an imposition on us but a reminder of what we should do, as a responsibility to all. If hiring this staff person provides the excuse to make the necessary changes, then so be it. But even if the firm does not hire this person for the position, making its office physically accessible should take precedence, since we never know when we or any staff member or client might need it.

Dubos's comment about survival has another meaning as well. We need to do all we can to accommodate the diverse abilities and perspectives of other people because, through that diversity, we gain the strength and understanding that we may need in order to survive. That may be obvious in a physical setting, where an inability to escape from an inaccessible building in the case of a fire, for example, can mean the difference between a person's life and death. But the existence of a diversity of differently abled people in an organization, like that of diverse plants or animals in an ecosystem, helps make it healthier, more resilient, and better able to survive whatever might come along.

There are many factors that go into a hiring decision, such as the one described here. But there is no question that we all benefit from increasing the diversity of people with whom we interact, the range of perspectives that we encounter, and the accessibility of the places in which we live and work. We learn the most from those who have overcome the most, whether physically disabled or challenged in some other way, and the more we open our minds to learn from them, the more able we will become as human beings and the more skilled we will become in overcoming whatever challenge confronts us.

## Firm Bankruptcy

**If thou suffer injustice, console thyself; the true unhappiness is in doing it.** —Democritus

**The principal of an architectural firm had known for several months that her firm might not survive. Although she had kept up appearances with her staff by meeting payroll, she had scrimped on other essentials, like paying herself or keeping up with the payment of rent and utilities at the office. At the point where she knew that she had no other choice but to declare bankruptcy and**

**close the office at year's end, she faced the question of when to tell her staff. Was it better to let them know right away so that they could start looking for other jobs, or to let them enjoy the holidays and have them discover the office closed at the start of the new year?**

We might all agree on the importance of honesty, but what about the timing of our honesty? Are there times when it is better not to be completely forthcoming in a particular situation, when not saying something to someone serves everyone's best interests? Does the timing of our speaking the truth make a difference in whether or not it constitutes honesty? If our frankness comes long after the absence of it has caused others harm, or after a longtime lack of candor, can we still call ourselves honest? Does honesty depend, in part, in being so at the very first opportunity, without hesitation or delay, or does its deployment depend on the context in which it occurs?

Such questions point to the difficulty of being honest, however simple that virtue might appear. They also point to the importance of the spatial and temporal setting in which virtuous acts happen, something that architects especially can appreciate as the shapers of space and time in the physical world. Spatially, honesty becomes more

difficult the closer we are to those with whom we need to be honest, since we have a better sense of how our comments will affect their feelings or future. We often have an easier time expressing a frank opinion about someone or something when we have little or no connection to them. It becomes much harder when we have long-standing bonds with a person or attachments to an object. In close relationships—with a spouse, friend, or coworker—knowing when to keep the truth to ourselves can make all the difference to keeping the connections healthy.

Honesty, in other words, exists within a sort of space-time continuum. As with our closeness to another, the timing of our openness also depends on our knowledge of its impact. Honest and potentially hurtful comments can prevent a person from hearing the substance of what we have said when delivered too hastily or at a point of particular vulnerability, in the same way that such comments, delivered too late, can seem like a betrayal of the trust that others put in us. The virtue of honesty relates, then, to other virtues, such as having good judgment and a sense of fairness in knowing when and where to convey a candid remark or to speak the truth.

In the case described here, honesty with coworkers about a looming bankruptcy and the loss of their jobs involves assessing when to reveal such upsetting news. Is ignorance bliss, as the saying goes, especially during the holiday season, or do our colleagues deserve to hear distressing information as soon as possible, particularly since they will need time to search for other work? The reciprocity principle of doing to others as you would have them do to you can help here. There may never be a universal measure of when and where to be honest; different people will respond to the truth in different ways. The best course may come from asking ourselves what we would want others to do were we in their position: would we want to be told of our impending layoff in the midst of a holiday?

The same reciprocity holds for those who eventually hear the news, whether sooner or later. We all have a natural reaction to resent those who cause our loss of a job, even if, as here, the boss has lost her job—and her business—as well. We may feel victimized when laid off, but we also need to remember, as Democritus suggests, the unhappiness of the bearer of bad tidings, especially when that person faces equal hardship. Every setback is an opportunity not just to take a new path in life but also to be honest with ourselves and not blame others for what lies beyond anyone's control.

# Firm Loyalties

> Take care of those who work for you and you'll float to greatness on their achievements. —H. S. M. Burns

**An architectural firm had a number of long-term, loyal staff members. A severe economic downturn led to the canceling of many of the office's projects, and the firm's partners faced the dilemma of whether to lay off most of the staff because of a lack of work or to find another way to cut payroll without layoffs. The staff offered to take pay cuts if the partners did the same, in hopes of riding out the downturn without people being fired, although some of the partners argued that it would be better to trim the staff and have fewer full-time people more committed to the firm's long-term health.**

The field of architecture has long had a cyclical nature, generally matching that of the construction industry. During building booms, most architects remain busy and do well, but during recessions, when new commissions can slow down dramatically, architectural offices often lay off staff as the remaining partners and principals hold on, if they can, until the next economic expansion. This process has all sorts of unintended consequences. It can cause a number of architecturally educated people to leave the profession entirely, which has had the unintended effect of greatly diversifying the career paths open to architects, who have found a demand for their creative skills in a number of sometimes only distantly related fields. The boom-and-bust cycles have also resulted in many architectural offices having large age gaps in their ranks, with a few older partners and many younger staff members. The number of middle-aged people in some offices seems small, often because members of that group had long ago left to start their own firms as a result of previous layoffs.

Laying off staff during an economic downturn has become so common as to seem normal and a sound business practice. After all, if revenue drops, an organization has to reduce its expenses accordingly, of which salaries constitute the largest part by far. But treating staff members as dispensable takes on a different meaning in a professional office, in which the knowledge and experience of its people constitute the greatest value a firm has to offer. When we see staff as a valuable investment rather than an expendable cost, it alters the decisions we might make when times get tough. Does it make sense, during an economic recession, to shed the real value of what we have to offer—our most experienced staff—or is it better to use employees' creativity and connections to find new work or imagine new services and revenue streams?

That may sound idealistic to the partner of a firm confronting a sudden shortfall in revenue. The quickest way to balance a budget involves eliminating salaries, and employment-at-will enables an employer to terminate staff without liability, unless a contract prohibits it. But what the law allows does not always align with what leadership demands of us. As H. S. M. Burns suggests, real leaders take care of their people first. Too many heads of organizations come to believe their organizational charts, which place them on the top of a pyramid of staff, when in fact the leaders of a firm or company belong at the bottom of an inverted pyramid, supporting all of their people above them, addressing the most difficult dilemmas that fall down to their level, and finding their fulfillment in the success of everyone above them. This demands a sense of selflessness and sacrifice that some who occupy positions of power do not have. The most successful organizations, though, remain those whose leaders take care of the people who work for them before taking care of themselves.

In the case of the firm finding itself with a sudden downturn in the amount of work in the office, such thinking would lead the leadership to pursue every other option before layoffs. It would demand open and honest conversations with staff members, enlisting them in finding ways to survive the downturn. It would also require that those in leadership positions make the greatest sacrifice, taking salary cuts as large or larger than those whom they employ. Most of all, it would entail making a commitment to taking care of every staff member as much as possible, perhaps finding other work for them to do and other positions they might fill. Such actions seem out of character in the competitive, capitalistic culture of the United States, but they serve organizations and people far better than the cycles of layoffs and hiring that mainly end up decreasing the value and productivity of the whole. Even in bad times, leaders who look after everyone else float to greatness, as Burns put it, in reputation if not always in revenue. And in the professional world, reputation is what counts.

## Untrustworthy Colleagues

**Those who trust us educate us.**

—T. S. Eliot

The founding partners of an architectural firm decided to retire at the same time and sell the business to a group of associates who had been with the firm for several years. Although this group agreed to gradually buy out the original partners, the new owners closed

# the office soon after completing the sale and started a new firm under another name, claiming that the economic downturn forced them to make this move and that they no longer had any financial obligations to their former bosses.

Loyalty and fidelity seem like quaint notions in a world that glorifies acting out of self-interest. Loyalty, as the philosopher Josiah Royce observed, involves the "thoroughgoing devotion of a person to a cause...beyond your private self, greater than you are." Such loyalty, of course, requires that the cause be just, as we have seen when people do horrendous things out of blind loyalty to groups such as the Nazis or the Taliban. Examples like that have made us justifiably wary of fidelity, even though such extremist groups show a complete infidelity to the most basic moral principles of compassion and dignity. But the other extreme—loyalty to no one but ourselves—remains equally destructive. Evident in the widespread infidelity of our time and the high rate of divorce that has resulted from it, personal disloyalty to others ultimately amounts to a form of self-destruction.

Such self-destruction becomes even more apparent when the disloyalty extends to our treatment of our colleagues, coworkers, and clients. When we enter into contracts with each other—whether between an employee and employer, a customer and a supplier, or a client and a professional—we do so with the belief that the other party will honor the agreement. Loyalty and legality share the same French root word—"loi"—and we trust that people will remain loyal to their contractual obligations, knowing that the law lies in wait for them if they do not. Disloyalty and the violation of others' trust, however much we may appear to benefit from them in the short term, always work against our best interests in the long run, for once others lose their confidence in us, it becomes hard to earn it back, far more difficult than to earn any amount of money or power. Therein lies the education that we receive when others trust us, as T. S. Eliot put it. Through their trust, we discover what it means to be trustworthy, and through their loyalty, what it means to be loyal in return, reciprocities without which society itself could not survive.

Fear often spurs people to act in untrustworthy or disloyal ways. As in the case of the new owners of a firm who walk away from the trust that the previous owners had placed in them to continue the practice and pay off their debts, economic survival led them to betrayal. With the economic downturn, paying the previous owners while also having to meet payroll and all of the other costs of doing business must have seemed overwhelming to the new owners. The ethical issues arise in how they decided to respond. Surreptitiously closing the old firm and starting a new one out of a misguided belief that that would relieve them of their fiduciary responsibility remain acts of extraordinary disloyalty.

The law can sort out the nature of the new owners' contractual obligations and resolve the financial issues in this case. But the greater harm comes from the ethical violation of the former owners' trust. Not only will the new owners likely never regain their former colleagues' confidence again, but the new owners may also have difficulty gaining the trust of the very people they most need it from: clients, colleagues, and coworkers. We distrust those who have behaved in untrustworthy ways, whether or not directly affected by their behavior, reasoning that if they betrayed others, they might someday do the same to us. The cost in terms of lost commissions, missed collaborations, and wary contributors far outweighs the cost of adhering to the original agreement, as difficult as it might have become.

This is where "loyalty to loyalty," as Royce said, becomes paramount. The new owners should have trusted the previous owners and their loyalty to their former firm, talking openly and frankly about the financial situation they all faced. Renegotiating the agreement, rewriting the conditions, and revisiting the payment amount and schedule with their former colleagues would have been a far better response for the new owners, for it would not only have reduced their long-term liability by avoiding possible litigation but would also have kept intact the most valuable asset they had: their trustworthiness. Ethics may seem less important than, say, economics or politics, but situations like this show that the right thing to do, ethically, is usually the best course, especially when it comes to money or power.

# 6

# Obligations to the Environment

**Members should promote sustainable design and development principles in their professional activities.**

# Environmental Hypocrisy

> **A hypocrite...professes what he does not believe.** —William Hazlitt

**A well-known advocate of sustainability, an architect who traveled extensively and lived in a sizable house, produced a large ecological footprint. When asked about the gap between his words and deeds, he said that he had no choice but to fly if he was to spread the word about environmental responsibility and that he had no guilt about living at a level commensurate with his income. Those who admired the content of his message, though, wondered what his life said about the difficulty of enacting his ideas.**

In the ancient world, philosophy was, as the historian Pierre Hadot put it, "a way of life," and ethics was a guide to living a good life. Thinking about right and wrong or good and bad did not just occur in philosophy classes but as an ongoing "spiritual exercise," said Hadot, in which ordinary people learned, via the ethics of philosophers such as Epicurus, to free themselves from "insatiable desires, by distinguishing between desires which are both natural and necessary, desires which are natural but not necessary, and desires which are neither natural nor necessary."

Hadot's work shows how far we have strayed from that ancient tradition of trying to live a good life. Philosophy has become the preserve of professors, who rarely try to communicate with the general public or offer much guidance as to what might constitute a good life in today's world. Nor do we expect professors to live according to what they profess, so accustomed have we become to hypocrisy, as William Hazlitt defined it: to people professing what they do not believe or will not do themselves.

Such hypocrisy extends to professions other than the professoriat. For the architect, whose work often involves realizing clients' desires and their images of a good life, the gap between what we profess and what we do can become extremely wide. The environmental dilemmas we face as a culture make that even more acute. Buildings consume a sizable amount of our financial, material, and energy resources, and they contribute mightily to the waste streams and greenhouse gases we generate. Most architects know that, yet we continue to design structures that, however efficient they may be in their operations or effective in reducing waste or pollution, still mainly serve the often insatiable desires of the wealthiest or most powerful portions of the population.

Nor do such desires stop with our clients. While virtually every architect now knows the impact and understands the implications of over-consuming resources and over-producing pollution, a strong desire remains within the profession to lead a life at least superficially similar to that of the wealthy or powerful people we serve. This may partly stem from a marketing motive. Architects, like any person in business, want to look successful as a culture conventionally defines that term, and living in exquisite surroundings can present a perfect advertisement of an architect's ability. But while it may be natural to want to live beyond our means, it is hardly necessary, no matter how much we try to justify it to ourselves.

If our desire for unsustainable luxury is both natural and unnecessary, architects also often end up entangled in activities rarely encountered in the ancient world but now common: the "unnatural but necessary." The unnatural part comes from modern technology and its ability to largely eradicate both spatial distances and temporal differences as we try to move everything from bits of information to human bodies as rapidly as possible around the world. Yet the necessary aspect of this arises from the need of people to connect and communicate with each other, even if, as in the case of the sustainability advocate here, that involves flying around to help others understand the price we pay for the "unnatural" power that our technology gives us. That places the proponents of a more environmentally friendly way of life in the paradoxical situation of generating a lot of greenhouse gases via automobile and airline travel to persuade others to generate a lot less.

The value of ethics lies not in making us feel guilty about our unnatural technology or unnecessary desires but in helping us find happiness in what comes naturally and in what is necessity. Seen in that light, ethics is a kind of design tool, a way to help people meet their needs in ways that they—and the rest of the planet—can support. The ancient Epicurean exercise of learning to want only what is both natural and necessary had the effect of helping people learn to live within what we would now call our ecological footprint.

Were our sustainability advocate to engage in the ethical exercises of the ancients, he might find more sustainable ways of working and living. He might video- or teleconference in lieu of face-to-face meetings, and record his messages rather than deliver them in person. He might also demonstrate, in his own lifestyle, how others can live with much less and still live well. And in so doing, he would reveal the ancient maxim at the core of sustainability: that a good life for all involves freeing ourselves from insatiable desires and finding happiness in living with what we absolutely need, to ensure that those who follow us have the same opportunity.

## Environmental Conflicts

Property is intended to serve life, and no matter how much we surround it with rights and respect, it has no personal being. It is part of the earth man walks on. It is not man. —Martin Luther King Jr.

An architect and a landscape architect, hired by a client to develop a high-end residential community in the foothills overlooking a pristine western

**landscape, discovered that the land crossed the migratory path of an endangered species. Blocking the migration route would threaten the very survival of the animal, whose numbers have been in steep decline in recent decades. The community, divided between wildlife lovers and property rights advocates, had to decide whether to allow the development to occur.**

Property rights have a particular resonance in a country like the United States. Thomas Jefferson, in writing the Declaration of Independence, used the word "happiness" in place of what the philosopher John Locke thought of as the essential rights of all people: "life, liberty, and estate [or property]." The equation of the pursuit of happiness and the right of property has deep roots in the American psyche, and it no doubt has had some effect on the low-density land use that has characterized much of the development in the United States since World War II. Owning a piece of land, however small and far from work, seems almost instinctual among many Americans. Such settlement patterns, however, have come to threaten our own mental well-being as well as the natural habitat of other species. And

they have led to daily commutes over such long distances that we might wonder just how different we really are from other migrating animals.

Many of the battles over property rights have occurred in newly developing areas, where conflicts have been most acute between those who claim to have an almost inviolable right to use their property as they see fit and those who see the need to balance this against the rights of others. Property-rights advocates point to the Fifth and Fourteenth Amendments to the U.S. Constitution, which call for just compensation for property taken for public use or through actions by the state. Some of the more extreme even see zoning laws as a taking of property by restricting some uses of it. But developments that meet all legal requirements, as in the case here, can still raise a difficult ethical question that even the most ardent property rights defender cannot avoid.

Do we have the right to eliminate something for all future generations or to drive another species to extinction? Such a question takes the property rights debate beyond that of conflicts between one person or group and another, to that of preventing to all who follow us the same rights, opportunities, and very existence that we have. Does the right to develop a piece of property trump the demise of a species or the interests of all future generations in its survival? If, as Martin Luther King Jr. said, property should serve life, then does the quantity, quality, and longevity of all life on a property matter more than the assumed right of owners at a particular point in time to do what they want with a piece of land?

While most conflicts over property rights end up in the courts, the ethical dilemmas behind them lend themselves to the "both-and" approach of design. In the case where a development will interrupt the migratory path of a declining species, that knowledge can lead to a court battle—or it can become a key determinant in the project's layout. There are, in other words, solutions other than a conventional development and no development at all. The architect and the landscape architect could design the development to locate roads and walks in such a way to avoid interfering with the animals' migration path.

A design approach to ethics, in other words, can help us get past polarized positions to accepting conflict as an essential part of creativity and recognizing competing interests as fundamental to finding new solutions. Unfortunately, the polarization often leads to legal battles that preempt the opportunity of designers to demonstrate possible alternatives to litigation. We need, instead, to declare our independence from these old patterns of bad behavior and start to pursue, through design, the liberty of our imagination, in the best interests of all life and with the well-being of other species in mind.

## Contextual Conflicts

Always design a thing by considering it in its next larger context—a chair in a room, a room in a house, a house in an environment, an environment in a city plan. —Eliel Saarinen

An architectural firm won a competition to design part of an Olympic site, which involved razing some of the city's historic urban fabric to accommodate and allow access to the sports facilities. The new development would provide a large amount of new public open space and new recreational facilities that would benefit the city long after the Olympics were done, but demolishing parts of the historic city also would eliminate much of the public realm and the neighborhoods that enabled community life to occur.

Licensed to look after the public good, architects have a clear responsibility to do so when private interests obviously harm the public realm, but that responsibility becomes less clear-cut when the conflict exists between two kinds of public good, as in this example. Although the public—including the global audience for the Olympics—benefits from the new facilities and park space, the public good involved in preserving the city's historic fabric also benefits many people, including future generations who will value the useful past of their ancestors. How do we determine which public good takes precedence? Should we have to choose?

In many ways, a conflict like this embodies a design failure, however brilliant the design of a project may be. As Eliel Saarinen observed, designers always need to take into account the next larger context of a project and to see everything we design in relationship to its surroundings, which are part of an even larger context. This recalls what the writer Arthur Koestler called the "holon," in which everything is at once a whole in itself and part of a larger whole. Koestler saw this as a way to get past the long-disputed dichotomy of atomistic and holistic approaches to reality, neither of which seemed able to capture the simultaneous, "both-and" nature of things. Design is inherently "holonistic." Every part of a project, from its smallest detail to its overall organization, comprises a series of sub-wholes, each of which has its own integrity yet is also part of a larger assembly, system, or composition. Likewise, a design failure occurs when we miss seeing something, however well designed in itself, as either a part of a larger whole or composed of smaller sub-wholes.

This runs counter to how we have organized much of our world as a series of discrete objects with little connection to larger wholes—whether other people, future generations, other species, or even ourselves at other points in time. Because of the "non-holonistic" way in which we have constructed our environment, we also suffer from myriad design failures that often take the form of unintended negative consequences: resource depletion, species extinction, habitat destruction, financial recession, and so on. Many think that we can solve such setbacks with a new technology or public policy aimed at correcting what went wrong before, but those too will fail without a new holon-based way to look at reality. Until we see the interconnected and interdependent nature of all reality, we will continue to lurch from one failure to another.

In the case of the Olympics site, the project, if well designed, would have provided the benefits of a new park and sports facilities within the city's historic fabric. Destroying the larger whole to accommodate a new part threatens both, for once the whole ceases to function, the parts will also not function well. The designer's responsibility lies not just in designing a beautiful, functional, and affordable whole but also in ensuring that that whole fits into the larger spatial and temporal context. That is not just a design idea, as Saarinen notes, but also an ethical idea, in that our responsibility, in whatever we do, lies not just at the scale at which we act but at the next larger scale as well. A good at one scale that leads to harm at another is no good at all.

> We think sometimes that poverty is only being hungry, naked, and home-less. The poverty of being unwanted, unloved, and uncared for is the greatest poverty. —Mother Teresa

**A**n architectural and engineering firm designed, for a poor country, a hospital that would use the anaerobic digestion of trash from local landfills as a source of energy. While environmentally responsible and cost effective, the process also affected the livelihood of a group of impoverished families who lived next to the landfill and made a subsistence income by recycling that same trash. This raised the question of whether the firm should switch to a more conventional energy source.

The utilitarian precept of doing what brings the greatest good to the greatest number, while seemingly simple, is far more complex than it first appears, especially in the case of competing goods, each of which brings different benefits to different groups. The common criticism of the utilitarian calculus of Jeremy Bentham lies in the ultimate inability of any of us to precisely calculate the full consequences of all of our actions. Meanwhile, reducing the number of variables to calculate the utility of something can get to the point of becoming meaningless or simply mean-spirited. Judging an action's goodness by its impact on those we can easily count leads to an ethics of those in power, for those in power, by those in power. This can increase the potential for ethical abuse in the name of ethics.

But an anticipatory mind—as opposed to a strictly mathematical one—can find in utilitarianism a useful tool for judging the merits of one good versus another. If the greatest number encompasses all beings currently and potentially alive, we can never actually count them, but we can imagine the impact of our actions on them and judge the ethics of a situation accordingly. Consider the case here, in which a firm has designed something good for its client, but not good for the people living off the landfill that will eventually fuel the client's facility. At first glance, the problem seems easily resolvable. The hospital has other sources of energy, while the impoverished recyclers presumably do not have other sources of income, or they would have likely chosen another, less desperate line of work. The architects and engineers on this project could

easily choose another fuel source and save the livelihood of a number of people in need.

However, when we expand our obligations to include all—every being currently and prospectively alive on the planet—utilitarian ethics leads to different conclusions. We cannot count the large number of those potentially affected by our actions, which may be why other species and future generations, let alone the currently poor, rarely get factored into our deliberations but we can imagine them and empathize with what they might want us to do in order for them to lead a decent life. Considering that empathetic imagination, we see that the greatest utility lies with those actions that enhance the ability of as many others as possible to thrive over the longest term. In the case of anaerobic digestion versus landfill preservation, the widespread and long-term benefits of recycling trash as an energy source, reducing the burden of our waste stream on future generations, and lowering the greenhouse gases emitted into the atmosphere outweigh the limited, short-term good of maintaining the subsistence of a relatively few number of impoverished families.

Not that the architects here can just ignore the plight of the people living off that landfill. As Mother Teresa observed, the poverty here is not just material—a matter of staving off hunger or homelessness—but also psychological and spiritual, the result of being unwanted, unloved, and uncared for. And many of us, by implication, impoverish ourselves by not wanting, not loving, and not caring for the poor. An ethics of empathetic imagination, in which we see the utility of benefiting as many others as we can, leads to what designers do all the time, often without even being asked: addressing as many of the anticipated needs in a situation with the fewest possible moves.

From that perspective, one solution to the hospital's energy system would involve not just installing an anaerobic digester but inaugurating a training program for those who formerly made their living off the local landfills to become the transporters and operators of the building's new recycling system. The digester's design, in other words, needs to extend beyond the technology itself. Turning trash into energy inside the hospital also presents an opportunity to heal a part of the larger community, transforming the untapped energy of people who have subsisted for too long on trash by caring for them and involving them in the reimagination of our collective future. That's healing.

## Future Generations

**Each generation imagines itself to be more intelligent than the one that went before it, and wiser than the one that comes after it.** —George Orwell

**An architect hired to add to a museum confronted the dilemma of a client who did not want to preserve an adjacent theater and a community who did want to see it saved. The architect showed the client how the addition could**

**be built in such a way that it reused the theater, as well as an office building next door. The client, however, decided to pursue the scheme that required demolishing both structures, relegating much of their materials to the landfill.**

Architects, like all professionals, have an obligation to a client to explore the options in a situation and to explain the implications of each. In so doing, professionals can and should make their preferences known, in how they weigh certain factors or assess certain risks, but in the end the client has the right to decide which option makes the most sense or seems the most appealing. It remains up to the professionals involved to decide whether they can live with that decision.

This becomes particularly difficult in assessing our collective obligations to past and future generations. A client often has needs that require attention right now, and so may not care much about preserving and reusing buildings from previous periods or about saving and conserving resources for future use. Nor does there exist many incentives for clients to do so. While the protests of preservationists may give some clients pause, property rights also give clients near total freedom to do what they want with their property within the law. Preserving things from the past or

conserving things for the future rarely plays into it, unless the project involves an already designated historic structure or if the site contains an already protected species.

George Orwell helped us see how we use language and the law to cover up unethical behavior. Property rights all too often become a way to disguise the wrongs we do to property, helping us feel good about ourselves as we damage or despoil what previous generations have left for us and what future generations might hope we leave behind for them. The property rights debate all too often revolves around the question of individual freedom versus governmental control. The real issue, however, has to do with ethics, with the debt we owe to those before us and obligations we have to those who follow us. Property rights are really about property responsibilities, about seeing ourselves as stewards of what we own, preserving what we have been given and improving on it, without depleting or damaging it, in order to pass it on.

That takes a degree of humility that Orwell thought we had lost in the modern world, captured in his sarcastic observation that we typically imagine ourselves to be more intelligent than our ancestors and wiser than our descendants. That remark suggests not only that we are neither more intelligent nor wiser than other generations but also that the one thing that our generation may have in abundance is hubris, the excessive pride and arrogance that almost invariably lead to tragedy. The modern era may be seen in the future as one of the most hubristic, and most tragic, of them all. We have, in the name of progress, demolished, desecrated, and defiled more of our resources than have most periods in human history, enabled by our technological prowess and fueled by a culture of overconsumption and condescension.

Design has certainly contributed to that culture. Design stars have often acted as if they had a divine right to demolish whatever lies in the way of their self-expression, and subservient designers have often accepted whatever a client decides, even if it destroys what is most valuable from past generations and most useful for future ones. Most of us become designers with the goal of improving the world, but our field has become so focused on the present, on who is hip and what is hot, that we too often forget to see our work and ourselves with much perspective. Were we to do so, we would recognize the Orwellian quality of so much of what we design.

A more intelligent path avoids both the self-delusion of celebrity and self-abasement of subservience. Instead, it speaks up for what is right and in the long-term interests of all involved in or affected by a project. In the case of this museum addition, the architect must present the solution that preserves the best of what already exists and conserves the most for the future, not just as one among many options but as the most responsible course of action. The client, of course, has the right to refuse, but if that happens, the architect also has the right—and should have the self-respect—to refuse to continue. Property rights really mean doing what is right for the property, not for the person who happens to own it at the moment. And, however inconvenient it might be to walk away from a job, we need to remind ourselves that future generations largely remember not those who maximized their own gain but those who stood up for others.

# Other Species

**An architect received a commission to design a building for a site that contained a well-established, diverse ecosystem. The clients wanted a substantial structure, one that would take up most of the zoning envelope and much of the site, requiring the clearance of most of the habitat already there. Surrounded by built-up development, the site was also one of the last remaining parcels of what was once a thriving natural landscape.**

Ethics, like architecture, has historically had an anthropocentric bias. Our responsibility to others extends to other people, both as human beings and as professionals, but rarely beyond that. Our contractual obligations reflect this bias, and owners are well within their rights to clear the site, as are architects well within their responsibility in doing what the zoning allows. But following zoning and obeying a contract does not make it right to destroy a thriving ecology. The loss of habitat on a single site may seem negligible, but each instance of environmental damage becomes, as

Jefferson observed, a lost link in a chain of nature that can eventually disappear, to the detriment of humans. We are the baby species, as some Native American cultures call us, unable to survive without the support of other plants and animals, most of whom can live quite nicely without us. We may think of ourselves as invincible, but that only hides our utter dependence on the planet we seem so intent on destroying.

Situations like this present architects with the paradox of having to eliminate a habitat for a number of other species to provide a habitat for our own. We create homes for ourselves in this way, which seems harmless at one scale, but utterly insane at another. What utility is there in evicting every other living being from a site in order for us to be there? Some utilitarians would answer that it has no utility at all, however pragmatic it may seem to clear a site prior to construction. By equating ethics with seeking the greatest good for the greatest number, utilitarianism raises the question of whom we include as part of the greatest number. In fact, on any given site, other species certainly outnumber us, so the most utilitarian approach demands that we attend to the greatest good of the great number of other species with whom we share the planet or at least a particular piece of property.

Given that, the architect's ethical obligation in this situation would be to find a way to accommodate her client's needs while also preserving or re-creating, to the greatest extent possible, the habitat for other species on the same site. That might entail showing how her clients can achieve what they want in a significantly smaller or more vertical house, to reduce the house's footprint on the site and allow more space for other species. Or it might involve maximizing the variety of plant and animal life on the property through the careful selection and planting of flora. The dilemma here is that there is almost no incentive to do so and almost every incentive not to. This is where ethics becomes an essential tool in helping us understand and then act on what is, in the end, in our best interest. In most design situations, we look at the particular circumstances and design accordingly, focusing on the specifics of a case. That parallels what philosophers call "act" utilitarianism, in which we determine the best thing to do by addressing the consequence of a particular action.

But "rule" utilitarianism takes a slightly different approach, and one potentially more useful here. It asks us to look at the consequences of following certain rules. Were all property owners to follow the rule that they have the right to clear their land of all flora and fauna, we would denude the landscape and damage our ability as humans to survive. A better rule, one with much better consequences for us as well as for others, would be to maximize the ecological diversity of every piece of property and thus our own resiliency as a species. While few zoning boards require that we follow such a rule, architects should require it of ourselves. Jefferson, one of the first architects in America, would certainly have agreed.

> **Our beginnings never know our ends.** —Harold Pinter

retail client hired a well-known architect to design a new product line. While the client did not ask him to do so, the architect decided to design each product so that it had a second use in addition to its primary function. When he showed the client his multi-use ideas, the retailer asked him why he had designed another use for everything, since that was not part of the brief, and he said that it was his way of countering a throwaway culture and encouraging people to keep products for a longer period of time. The client liked the cleverness of the designs, but worried that this would end up reducing the number of items customers would purchase as a result.

Design remains one of the most fundamental of human activities. Long before we had recorded history or established civilizations, humans made things to accomplish some end, some purpose essential to our surviving or thriving. People often falsely distinguish between "engineering" and "design," thinking the former focuses solely on function and the latter solely on form, as if pragmatics and aesthetics occupy two different realms of human activity. Even the most cursory knowledge of design, however, shows that, unlike fine artists, for whom form can serve as an end in itself, designers always balance form and function, aesthetics and pragmatics. Any attempt at divorcing the two will lead to bad design—and poor engineering.

But design also constitutes a creative activity, going beyond simply creating merely functional objects and environments to envisioning new ways to live and work in the world. The best designs do not just meet our expectation; they exceed them and enable us to do something or to be someone more than we could in the past. While all design begins with a "brief," a list of the requirements the design needs to fulfill, great design ends up meeting the brief while also reinterpreting it, expanding it, or seeing in it opportunities that the writer of the brief had not noticed or imagined. As the playwright Harold Pinter says, we never know where the creative process will end up.

This requires, though, not just an inventive designer but also an open-minded client, one willing to seize the opportunity that good design creates and to recognize that the greatest benefit accrues to those who generate a functioning form that, once it exists, we cannot imagine living without. Unfortunately, the world seems to have far fewer clients with such openness to new ideas than it does designers. You only have to look at the myriad projects lying unbuilt and in a drawer in every designer's office to see how far the supply of ingenuity and inspiration exceeds the demand. More untapped profit exists in the offices of designers than in all the balance sheets in our banks and boardrooms.

The case of the double-duty line of products offers just such an example. Although not asked by the client to design the products to be multipurpose, the designer saw the potential of this line of goods to reinvent how we use things and the speed with which we dispose of them. It also questioned the belief implicit in our consumer culture that the faster people throw things away, the greater the potential profit for a manufacturer and a retailer. The very fact that such planned obsolescence has become so accepted meant that it offered the most opportunity for the designer to rethink it and show how even greater gains accrue when we take into account people's proclivity to prize their possessions and not constantly have to dispose of them to buy something new.

It takes courage, of course, to do something like this: courage on the designer's part to do more than was asked for in the brief and courage on the client's part to entertain an unanticipated end result. The easiest response, when faced with uncertainty, is to fall back on the familiar. The client in this case may have thought that, in hiring a well-known designer, the company would get some-thing predictable, similar to what this designer had done successfully before. But the renown of the best designers comes from their not doing the expected, but instead from creating things no one had thought of before and no one can now imagine living without. In that sense, design remains not only one of the most fundamental human activities

but also one of the activities that most reminds us of what it means to be human, ending up in places we never could have imagined when we started. In this case, the company decided against producing this new product line. By fearing to go where it had not intended, however, the organization took a step toward it's own planned obsolescence, the very thing it seemed so fearful of losing.

## Reducing Consumption

To maintain one's self on this earth is not a hardship but a pastime, if we will live simply and wisely.

—Henry David Thoreau

An architect regularly spends her first session with clients analyzing their needs and trying to talk them out of doing most of what they had requested by showing them why it might be unnecessary or too costly and how they can achieve

**their goals more sustainably. Other architects thought she was foolish to attempt to persuade clients to do as little as possible, since her fees were based on the size of the buildings she designed, although she also seemed to have no lack of clients eager to work with her and no lack of money to support the modest life she leads.**

At the heart of every profession should lie its own version of medicine's Hippocratic oath to do no harm. In architecture, that ethic poses a particular challenge because buildings, among the largest objects humans make, have a significant social, economic, and environmental impact almost out of necessity. Doing *no* harm may remain a goal, but one rarely achieved in a field that currently uses almost half the energy and water that humans consume and gives off almost half the greenhouse gases that humans generate. Many architects have embraced energy efficiency and carbon reduction strategies in their designs, but few do what the architect in this case has done: try to reduce the overall quantity of what we build and inhabit. The economic incentives to do so do not exist, as the more buildings and the larger the

buildings, typically the higher the architects' fees. Nor does the culture—both within the profession and in the larger society—reward such behavior. Modest structures remain mostly ignored by the media and the masses.

Dramatically reducing the amount of space, materials, and energy we consume, however, must stand as the best step we can take to sustain ourselves not just environmentally but also personally, as Thoreau observes. We work more to have more, but because we work more, we do not have the time or energy to enjoy the more we have. Architects, whose professional culture has mythologized long hours and "all nighters," may rank among the worst in terms of finding a work-life balance, even as others increasingly turn to our field for advice on how best to live sustainably. All of that makes the dissuasion of the architect here so unusual. What may seem not in her best interest may be, by far, the best thing for the planet and for her clients, and as a result, the best thing for her—or any architect—to do.

Architects do not just accommodate the needs of specific clients and communities but also exemplify through our buildings and our own lives how we believe people should live. Most architects do not think about their work as promoting a particular view of what comprises a good life, but most members of the public understand that, at least intuitively, as is evident in their reactions to buildings and to our behavior. While we often overly intellectualize what we do, the public typically responds in more intuitive, ethically charged ways: calling something good or bad, right or wrong, beautiful or ugly with a directness most architects will avoid.

That points to the gap that can open up between what we say and what we do. We might say all we want about making buildings or communities more sustainable, but if we design more than people need, more than the budget allows, or more than the planet can bear, our words will mean nothing. If, however, we live simply and wisely, to use Thoreau's terms, and aim all of our effort at helping others do the same, we will find that maintaining ourselves is not a hardship but a pastime. That is what this architect's practice implies. Her efforts to talk people out of doing too much—or much at all—may seem self-defeating to her colleagues, but she will never lack for meaningful work, nor will her clients ever lack the means of living a sustainable life. What she offers her clients and exemplifies in her own practice is what many ethicists have long supported: live with less and we will have more—more happiness said the Hedonists, more contentment said the Stoics, more time for study and contemplation said the Aristotelians and Platonists.

Modern architecture started down that path and then lost its way, allowing the principle of "less is more" to become an excuse for the use of extravagant materials, expensive details, and excessive space. The postmodern reaction to this—"less is a bore"—only shifted the overindulgence to a surfeit of materials, ornament, and form while hastening the irrelevance of architects to all but the relatively few well-off enough to afford such excess. Ethics offers us another way—another way to practice and design, in which we focus on what people, and the planet, really need and then provide that in as elegant and economical a way as possible. Then, and only then, will we start to approach the principle of doing no harm.

In law a man is guilty when he violates the rights of others. In ethics he is guilty if he only thinks of doing so. —Immanuel Kant

A civil engineering firm with landscape architects on staff received a commission by a riverside city prone to flooding to upgrade its storm water drainage system, including higher floodwalls that would move storm surges faster downriver. The landscape architects in the firm offered an alternative that involved restoring wetlands upriver to absorb storm water and reduce surges. The communities downriver preferred the wetlands solution, while landowners of low-lying land objected to their property being taken for conversion to wetlands.

Many of the conflicts that occur in the public realm revolve around the question of private property, and the extent to which trumps the other: the government's interests or the property owner's rights? The answer to such conflicts often lies somewhere between the two extremes. We have resolved, through zoning and other regulations, that owners cannot do whatever they want with their property, especially if it adversely affects the property of others, just as we have decided that the government cannot seize property without due process and compensation to the owner for its fair market value.

The debate over property rights and the public interest, however, tends to overlook the larger context in which both occur: the natural environment. There are environmental regulations, of course, that have become points of contention among property rights advocates, in part because ecosystems link property owners in webs of relationships far more complex than our neat partitioning of the land can accommodate. But even environmental regulations rarely go as far as the new Constitution of Ecuador, the first to recognize the rights of nature as equivalent to those of humans.

As that Constitution says, "Nature...has the right to exist, persist, maintain and regenerate its vital cycles, structure, functions, and its processes in evolution. Every person, people, community, or nationality, will be able to demand the recognition of rights for nature before the public bodies." This gives new meaning to the distinction that Kant makes between the law and ethics, between how we act toward and how we think about the rights of others. By recognizing the rights of nature, Ecuador has created law that has the greatest ethical scope possible.

Many might dismiss Ecuador's recognition of ecosystem rights as having little legal relevance to people in other countries, despite the fact that this constitution gives people of any nationality the right to argue for the rights of nature before public bodies. But this recognition of nature's rights has, given Kant's distinction, great ethical and practical relevance. Ethics, unlike the law, doesn't respect national boundaries; American ethics doesn't differ in any fundamental way from Ecuadorian ethics. And the idea of nature having rights equal to that of humans, as Kant might say, makes even thinking of violating those rights unethical.

This is so not only in theory, but also in practice. As the case described here suggests, respecting the rights of nature aligns with respecting the rights of humans, who are, after all, a part of nature. Using the natural systems of wetlands to deal with storm surges, as the landscape architects propose, not only reduces the ever-increasing costs of heavy infrastructure to alleviate the threat of flooding, but also acknowledges the rights of communities downriver who are adversely affected by the city passing its flood problem on to others by accelerating flood waters rather than absorbing them.

Respecting the rights of nature appears to conflict with the rights of property owners who want to alter habitat and affect ecosystem health in order to achieve human ends. While that conflict seems real, it is not. Property is as inseparable from nature as humans are, and destroying ecosystems also destroys the value of the property in those ecosystems, whether property owners realize it or not. Likewise, enhancing the health of ecosystems raises the value of the property within it, even if those ecosystems contain a relatively large measure of native habitat and less human intrusion that we have become accustomed to.

As Kant says, we are guilty of unethical behavior if we think of violating the rights of others—other species as much as other people—and since those other species have as much right to habitat as humans do, we have an ethical responsibility to accommodate both. The wetland proposal not only recognizes the property rights of people downriver—of people indirectly affected by our decisions—but also recognizes the rights of other species who

regain habitat with every wetland we restore.

Even if American law doesn't (yet) recognize the rights of nature as extensively as Ecuador's constitution does, our laws do recognize the violation of the rights of other people and those end up in the same place, our larger scale of reference. Because ecosystems link us all, almost any negative impact on a particular piece of property eventually has an adverse effect on other property. Likewise, enhancements to the ecosystem of a property almost invariably enhance that of others. And using nature's infrastructure, its water courses and wetlands, to handle whatever nature sends our way is the best way to protect everyone's property, human and non-human alike.

## Postscript: Why Ethics Matters Now

In a depressed economy, ethics may seem extraneous: something nice to do once we pay the bills. But the opposite is true. During difficult times, questions at the heart of ethics, such as what constitutes a good life, become uppermost in most people's minds. Economic downturns, for all of the pain they bring, also overturn unsustainable assumptions and disrupt unrealistic aspirations, leading people to ask what really matters and wonder what they really want.

The more architects embrace ethics in times like these, the more in-demand we will be. Fewer clients may be able to commission buildings, but far more people now need help in redefining what is essential, what they can do without, and what gives them happiness. Architects' roles become less about designing buildings and more about envisioning a more sustainable, affordable, and equitable future. And we need to exemplify that in everything we do—in how we treat people as well as in how we build structures for them to live, work, and play in. As practitioners of the most public art, we need to align our architecture with our values, since, in the end, we cannot help others achieve a good life if we cannot practice such a life ourselves.